RETURN FROM THE EDGE

MICHAEL WILSON

CONTENTS

RETURN FROM THE EDGE

By Michael Wilson

© 2019 Michael Wilson

Print ISBN 978-1-7339405-3-5

Published by: The Ghost Publishing

DEDICATION

I'm dedicating this book to my beautiful mother. I believe this book, as well as many accomplishments I've been honored to be a part of, wouldn't have been possible without the support of my mother.

My mother's unwavering support is unseen in this book. You will witness her achievements, through me, by applying the teaching I share in this book to your life.

Understand that, even though she's not mentioned very often, her unwavering support, strength, devotion, and sacrifices did not go unnoticed.

A mother's love for her children goes unspoken more times than not. However, a mother shows her love through her gentle touch, her loving actions.

I'm also eternally grateful to Aunt Barbara. She has sacrificed her time, without complaint, these past twelve years when medical adversities mandated action.

Special thanks goes out to many family members, as well as friends, who've met the many challenges that have presented themselves over my life.

— Mike Wilson

FOREWORD

I have known Mike since he was a star basketball player in WV. He is a man who, by God's grace, survived a terrible, crippling wreck. I was his pastor for several years and I watched him struggle, but not give up on life nor his divine destiny. He pressed on and became a man who has a heart to help encourage others. He is a man who loves Jesus with all his heart. His book was written to help all who struggle in any area of their lives — physically, emotionally, and most of all, spiritually.

— DR. JAMES WRIGHT, FOUNDING PASTOR
OF THE MARANATHA FELLOWSHIP
CHURCH AND FULL-TIME EVANGELIST
AND MENTOR

~

Winner, winner, winner! This is the word that describes Mike Wilson.

There is something deep inside us that requires a meeting with God's power. Our potential is inside us, merely awaiting activation. God's power calls out the supernatural, God's power commissions your ability to accomplish the impossible, summons you to go deeper and catapults you to new heights. Mike has teamed up with God to overcome his struggles... along with great amounts of support from family and friends.

He has had great "storms" in his life and has come back every single time. Mike is an inspiration to all who know him and even those who encounter him. He lives his life from a wheelchair, having once been a terrific athlete. One trip, as a passenger in a speeding car, cost him severely.

But, God wants Mike to know Him by making him known through his personality, passions, gifts and experiences. Just an incredible story of perseverance, love, belief, and actionable steps to overcome a tremendous adversity.

So inspirational.

— COACH GREG WHITE, FORMER HEAD BASKETBALL COACH AT UNIVERSITY OF CHARLESTON, MARSHALL UNIVERSITY, AND UNIVERSITY OF PIKEVILLE. ASSISTANT BASKETBALL COACH UCLA, MARSHALL UNIVERSITY. MOTIVATIONAL SPEAKER, 1979—PRESENT, OWNER OF GREGWHITESPEAKS.COM

Mike Wilson has a story that all of us, especially teenagers and young adults, need to hear. I have seen him speak at high schools. His powerful story captures the attention, hearts, and minds of those who truly listen.

When Mike explains how a single decision can affect the rest of your life, he does so from a wheelchair. Turning tragedy into triumph has been incredibly difficult. He has had plenty of health problems and emotionally low periods to overcome. Through his strong faith and the love and support of family and friends, Mike – a fine athlete in his youth — has persevered and met every challenge he's had to face. With his positive attitude of gratitude, as well as his wonderful, friendly spirit and sense of humor, Mike's story will touch and inspire you.

This book can help you overcome your own situation when facing difficult or tragic circumstances in your life.

— TIM DIPIERO, ATTORNEY, DIPIERO
SIMMONS MCGINLEY & BASTRESS, PLLC,
CHARLESTON, WEST VIRGINIA

PREFACE

After a life-altering car accident, I found myself confined to a wheelchair for life. This book will not only take you on my personal journey of recovery, but will supply you with tools to help you overcome whatever you are struggling with, whether it be an emotional, physical, or mental issue.

As you read this book, the words will not only become real to you in many ways but will offer insightful methods on how achieving success can benefit you. These methods contain the keys to unlock the windows of your soul.

— *MIKE WILSON, AUTHOR*

INTRODUCTION

In a world of more than 8 billion people, I'm one of the few that do what I do. I get excited about encouraging others. I love when they take what I say to heart and start taking action in living the lives of their dreams. I love stimulating hope and courage into the hearts of those who have all but quit on themselves. Too many people have taken a back seat to who they have the potential to be or never had the confidence to explore how great they can become.

While there are many "motivational speakers," what makes me stand out a little more is that when the other speakers stand in front of an audience, I sit.

I'm in a wheelchair. I suffered a spinal injury that left me with paralysis from my chest down. When I roll up on the stage, just by them seeing me gives them hope that they can do more than what they've done. I wasn't born with paralysis. I was an athlete. I joined the Navy. But something happened early in my life that permanently put me in a chair.

I can't tell you the darkness I've had to walk through to become who I am today. It was a journey I had no idea I was strong enough to finish. I have gone through many experiences, not as an able-bodied individual but as someone living with a significant disability. Now that I'm on the other side, I have a message for everyone else – What can't you do?

Interaction with audiences or when I coach people one-on-one brings me joy, and it gives me a sense of purpose. I never thought I could get here, but today I am walking or rolling in my purpose, and I love it.

There are five central pillars of life that I help people with. I help people focus on them and give them tools and techniques to master them. Although I'm a big-picture guy, when I teach, I teach small, incremental steps anyone can do to have a better life.

Five environments we find ourselves in life.

1. Living: What is your current living environment? Are you satisfied with it?
2. Learning: How do you best learn? Even as an employee or student, how do you continue to progress in your job performance? Are you figuring out how to start your own business?
3. Financial: Do you like where you are financially? Your best thinking got you there. How do you define success? Is it financial independence? Are you struggling paycheck to paycheck?
4. Social: Who do you socialize with? Do you have healthy relationships or ones that bring harm to you in any way? What do you think people think of you? Would you like to change it?
5. Spiritual: Your faith. We all have a belief system; it can either keep you well or not. Faith in God, the universe, or yourself.

Most people have the fuel inside them but just need a spark. One small but intense spark can turn into a forest fire. Changing the trajectory of just one person's life can impact thousands.

CREDIBILITY

I can't express the loss, shame, frustration, and pity I felt after losing the ability to walk. I've gone through lonely and intense dark times; trust me, it wasn't fun. However, it was necessary. Out of the ashes came a compelling desire not to let my accident define me. In 2016 I earned a degree in Rehabilitation Studies. I'm now qualified not only to help people rehabilitate their lives but also to help addicts and people who have been through traumatic experiences.

When I roll onto a stage and speak, it's not just from my personal experiences, it's from tried and true scientific methods on how people can rid themselves of limiting beliefs and transform into people they are proud to be.

I wish I had a book like this when I was going through intense, emotional pain. In the same way, I hope this book falls in the hands of the person who is not happy with him or herself but does not know how to turn things around. I hope it falls into the hands of others with a disability so they can steamroll over the limitations they or others have put in front of them.

I am glad God made way for it to fall into your hands. I don't believe in coincidences. I believe you were meant to read it because you are meant to do more with your life. As you see my journey, your own will be revealed to you. It starts with one simple step... turn the page.

PART ONE

LIFE-ALTERING EVENTS

"Never, never, never, never give up."

— *WINSTON CHURCHILL*

LIFE, WITHOUT GOALS, IS LIKE A CAPTAIN STEERING HIS SHIP on the open seas — without coordinates. It'll get somewhere but he has no idea where that may be. Goals are important; they are what keep us on track to do what's important in our lives. However, not all goals are easily met. In fact, many goals are never reached. It can be our own fault that we don't succeed, or it can be through extenuating circumstances, things you have no control over.

Maybe you've experienced a life-altering event. It could have been an emotionally devastating period in your life, such as a divorce, or unexpected termination from work. You might be physically broken, either from disease or an accident. Maybe you've been psychologically scarred... for years. Or maybe you're spiritually wounded, wondering why God would allow terrible things to happen to good people.

Regardless of the circumstances, you — or someone you know — has been broken. Like a glass dropped to the floor, your life has shattered. You're left with hundreds of pieces, wondering how all those fractured shards can be put back together. Wondering if they'll ever be put back together and made whole again.

If you've fallen into a pit of despair, this book is for you. If you're teetering on the edge of the pit — if you're hanging onto a semblance of a normal routine, if you're wondering how long you can continue plodding along, pretending everything is fine... this book is for you.

My goal is to bring you, the walking wounded, keys to recovery, motivation, encouragement, wellness tools, and most importantly: hope.

Recovery can't be summed up with a few meaningless platitudes. If you've been the recipient of well-meaning, but empty comfort, you understand the frustration. A pat on the arm or a hug followed by a sincere, "I know how you feel," or "It will all look better in the morning," or "Everything happens for a reason," doesn't help your situation. Realize that those people just don't know what to say. They are not living with your circumstances. They really don't know how you feel. In this book, I am not offering trite, over-used, empty cheeriness to temporarily boost your mood.

I've been there — where you are now. I've experienced total devastation in my life. My future went from being on track with goals and dreams, to utter desolation.

Follow along on my journey; from training as an athlete, from a life filled with promise as a serviceman in the United States Navy to adapting to life in a wheelchair and learning how to recover.

THE EARLY YEARS

Growing up in Braxton County, West Virginia, my parents gave my brother and me a healthy, normal childhood. We regularly attended a Baptist church; we rode bikes all over town; we played basketball and baseball. My parents loved us enough to uproot their lives and move to Charleston, West Virginia, so my brother, Todd, and I could attend a better Christian school.

Dad instilled a strong work ethic in us from a young age. He set up a small lawn mowing business in the summers. I was in the seventh grade, and Todd was in the sixth grade. Between the two of us, we had twenty-five lawns to cut weekly. Dad transported us and the lawnmowers from house to house. He'd cut other lawns as well. We kept those lawnmowers cutting grass whenever possible.

That part-time job gave us kids spending money. We'd save for special things we needed (or wanted) for the upcoming school year. When Air Jordans came out, I wanted them, but special basketball shoes weren't in the family's back-to-school budget. At the time, they cost $64. I saved for them and my parents paid for half. I cherished those shoes.

Other times, Mom might say something like, "We've got twenty dollars to make it to payday." With two growing boys and two adults, money was tight. Dad got paid on Fridays. So, fairly often, that lawn-mowing money came in handy.

In Braxton County, we both played on sports teams in school. We made it to the All-Stars tournament while there. In the fourth and fifth grades, I wanted to play football, but you had to be in the seventh or eighth grade to participate.

In order to play in a varsity game when I was in the seventh grade, I'd have to play against kids at least a year older than me.

A LESSON ON ATTITUDES IN LIFE

When I was in the eighth grade, a sign hung on the wall of the locker room. It read, "Attitude is Everything." If each team member's attitude is in the right spot, everyone achieves more. If someone had good skills but a lousy attitude, they probably wouldn't even make the team.

In 2008, with forty-one seconds on the clock, the Florida Gators football team only needed one yard to make a first down, giving them a chance to win the game. They didn't make the yard and consequently, they lost. After the game, Florida Gators starting quarterback, 1Tim Tebow, spoke on national TV. His remarks have since become known as the memorable "I Promise" speech.

"To the fans and everybody in Gator Nation, I'm sorry, extremely sorry. We were hoping for an undefeated season. That was my goal, something Florida's never done here. But I promise you one thing, a lot of good will come out of this. You will never see any player in the entire country play as hard as I will play the rest of the season, and you will never see someone push the rest of the team as hard as I will push everybody the rest of the season, and you will never see a team play harder than we will the rest of the season. God bless."

That speech was very inspirational for his team. Tim went on to lead the Gators on a ten-game winning streak, taking the SEC championship, and winning the national championship. His determination not only spurred his team to greatness, it has continued to inspire many sports teams and individuals to try a little harder to push for success.

I had my own lesson in pushing for success. While in junior high, during Christmas break, the schedule announced there was no JV basketball practice. Only the varsity team would practice that day. So, I decided to sleep in. I played JV, why would I go to the varsity practice?

Later, the coach asked me, "Where were you?"

I answered honestly. "There wasn't a practice for JV, so I slept late."

He came back at me. "So, aren't you on the JV team?"

"Yes, sir. I am."

"Would you like to make the varsity team next year?"

"Yes, Sir, I would."

His answer was simple. "You should have been there."

Even though the varsity team was bigger than me. Even though they picked on me and were too rough on me. Even though I wasn't playing at their level, Coach's message was simple: *Don't miss an opportunity for self-improvement.*

He said, "The thing is, to get better, you have to compete at *that level* — that's what it takes."

Coach may not remember saying that to me, but I remember. He taught me about not making excuses, about commitment, determination, perseverance, and teamwork. Never giving up and sacrificing my own needs and wants for the team helps to compete *at that level.*

At that point, college basketball was my goal. I was good at sports, especially basketball and baseball. I learned life lessons, like complaining to the ref wasn't going to change the score. That taught me that complaining about problems won't solve anything. Sports and sportsmanship taught me about personal responsibility at an early age.

Everybody has different experiences in life, but, at some point, you have to use tools to achieve progress.

I HAD NO IDEA HOW MUCH I WOULD NEED THOSE LIFE LESSONS

As you'll read, I've had more than my fair share of devastation. I have met despair, eaten with it, slept with it, and bathed in it. I have seen darkness that would probably engulf others without a way of escape. Despair is a terrible feeling. Devastating, debilitating, trauma is as hard on the human mind and spirit as there is. When you encounter complete despair, you're between a rock and a hard place. You can't hide from yourself.

I'm writing this book to tell you, when in the midst of the despair, you can find a way to be strong, or put on a brave face. Alone in the dark, facing our insurmountable dilemma, having faith in God is literally the only resource available.

During my pit of despair, a verse from the Bible, Romans 8:28, came to my mind every night.

And we know that God causes all things to work together for good to those who love God, to those who are called according to His purpose.

— ROMANS 8:28

When life throws us a curve ball, when things can't get any worse, have faith. Have faith it will get better. Have faith in yourself. Most of all, have faith in the Lord.

2

PURSUING DREAMS

"Things change. And friends leave. Life doesn't stop for anybody."

— *STEPHEN CHBOSKY*

IN THE EARLY 1990S, AS A YOUNG ADULT, I CHANGED direction in my career goals. Seldom does a young person determine and not stray from a set path for their life's trajectory. Only a rare child prodigy, such as Marie Curie or Mozart, has been gifted early in life with an overriding focus and drive. The rest of us try to figure out our inclinations for a career as we mature and develop. Sometimes, our life's path deviates or influences our plans. Sometimes, those eleventh-hour deviations can bring about major changes in our lives.

While attending Fairmont State University, an NCAA Division II institution, I became restless. Even though I'd always loved sports and was playing the best basketball I had in my whole life, I left Fairmont State after barely a semester. I wasn't happy there. The coach told me they would only keep two *walk-ons*, meaning I wasn't going to receive any scholarship money.

The school was an hour and a half from home, so I'd lived on campus and away from family. The school, during those years, didn't have enough of a well-known basketball reputation to attract professional recruiters.

I quickly concluded that, at Fairmont, my sports dreams were only a pipe dream.

The colleges drawing attention were schools like Duke, UNLV, the University of Arkansas, the University of North Carolina, the University of Indiana, and the University of Kentucky. I lived in West Virginia, so attending any of the top basketball colleges was out of reach for me.

In the winter of 1990, I left Fairmont and came back home. It was too late to begin spring classes at West Virginia State College, so I planned to register for fall classes. That left me with a few months to work, wait, and plan.

My dream was to graduate, majoring in criminal justice, with an end goal of entering a police academy or, depending on my GPA, head straight into a job with the DEA or the FBI. Working in law enforcement had always been a strong ambition of mine.

In the spring of 1991, my brother Todd decided to pursue a career in medicine. He approached military recruiters, who visited us at home on three separate occasions. Todd was a year younger than me and needed our parents' consent to join the military. He planned to become a hospital corpsman and, later, continue with further medical training. During the recruiters' talks, they noticed me and, of course, included me in the discussions. They didn't have to really talk to hard for me to sign up. Ultimately, I chose to serve my country rather than play basketball.

Sports had always meant a lot to me — but keeping America's freedom secure held a higher calling. It drew on my instincts to protect people from the oppressors of the world, in the same way a career in law enforcement would.

Todd and I both worked at Chick-fil-A and mowed lawns

while we made progress toward our career goals. That spring, I was nineteen, and he wasn't quite eighteen.

Just prior to our military interest, a movie had been released, *Navy SEALs*, starring Charlie Sheen and Bill Paxton. While it wasn't as big of a box office success as *Top Gun* (1986, starring Tom Cruise) had been, it influenced me. The movie hit at the right time in my life. The 1984 release of Lee Greenwood's song, "God Bless the U.S.A." (also known as "Proud to Be an American"), enjoyed continuous popularity and playtime on radios. The song gained greater prominence during the Gulf War, in 1990 and 1991, and stirred up patriotism in Americans. I was one of those Americans.

It had been a while since the U.S. had engaged in a war. The Vietnam War ended in 1975, so it was the first real conflict that was able to be nationally televised. It was referred to as "The First Television War." Walter Cronkite, with "The CBS Evening News," brought film of the war into America's living rooms. By that time, most homes in the U.S. had TVs, even though most were black and white sets.

Fast forward to 1990. Iraq invaded Kuwait on August 2nd of that year. The website, 1Infoplease.com, in an article, "The Persian Gulf Wars," discusses The Gulf War:

Operation Desert Storm was launched on Jan. 18, 1991, under the leadership of U.S. Gen. Norman Schwarzkopf.

The U.S.-led coalition began a massive air war to destroy Iraq's forces and military and civil infrastructure. Iraq called for terrorist attacks against the coalition and launched Scud missiles at Israel (in an unsuccessful attempt to widen the war and break up the coalition) and at Saudi Arabia. The main coalition forces invaded Kuwait and S Iraq on Feb. 24 and, over the next four days, encircled and defeated the Iraqis and liberated Kuwait. When U.S. President George H.

W. Bush declared a cease-fire on Feb. 28, most of the Iraqi forces in Kuwait had either surrendered or fled.

～

I'D BEEN a young child during the Vietnam War, but, by 1990, I was a grown man. The world watched as the United Nations took action. A coalition of thirty-nine nations, including the United States, Britain, Egypt, France, and Saudi Arabia joined forces. When the U.N. Security Council called for Iraq to withdraw, U.S. troops moved into Saudi Arabia to protect Saudi oil fields. The United Nations set a deadline for the withdrawal of Iraqi troops from Kuwait. When Saddam Hussein refused to comply, Operation Desert Storm began.

By 1990, we were well past watching the news on black and white televisions. *The Information Age* had begun. People were aware of situations much faster than in previous generations. Radio stations gave regular updates on skirmishes in the Middle East. An estimated 42% of Americans had access to a computer.

CNN had established itself as the first all-news network. They were the only source that could communicate from Iraq during the beginning of the American bombing campaign. They broadcast live reports from inside Iraq.

No longer did Americans have to wait for the evening news to hear what was going on in the world. Now we had front-row seats. America took an active interest in The Gulf War. I had an active interest in The Gulf War – I had family there and my patriotism had been roused. I was ready to serve my country.

My cousin, Eric, worked as a mechanic on Apache helicopters; his battalion was sent to Iraq early on. By the time Eric came home from the Middle East, about seven months later, I had been signed, sealed, and delivered to the Navy to train as a SEAL in San Diego, California. I'd met their rigorous physical, mental, psychological, and emotional requirements for SEAL training.

Another cousin and I joined the military together, though neither of us obtained a guaranteed "A" school contract. I was ready to go; I didn't want to delay any longer. We would have had to wait probably six months to be guaranteed an A-school contract.

A Navy Class "A" School is where you go after boot camp to receive your primary job training. In the fifth week of boot camp, you should receive an "A" school decision. You may not be given your first choice of schools, due to qualifications, job availability, or other reasons, but you should receive your second or third choice. That's what I was told.

Since there were no guarantees for anyone completing SEAL training, I had to choose three fallback career choices. I selected military police (which still applied to my original field in college — criminal justice), diver, or heading into combat.

However, during my fifth week of boot camp, I was told the only available school was Mess Specialist – they called the job *a chef*. No matter what name it went by, it was still cooking. So, they were offering me, as a fallback schooling plan, a military career as a cook instead of becoming a SEAL, an M.P., a diver, or even heading into combat. They wanted me to learn how to prep food, cook, bake, and basically, feed people as a job. That was not something I'd joined the Navy to do. Meaning no disrespect to people who are chefs, cooks, or bakers, but it was not the career for me. I don't even cook for myself at home, and if I ever attempted it, I'm sure nobody would want to eat my cooking.

During SEAL training, about one in four recruits succeed and move on to secure a position in BUD/S training (BUD/S is an acronym for Basic Underwater Demolition/SEAL). BUD/S is a long, extensive, and exhaustive training. They condition already-fit men and women to build more stamina; they train candidates in areas such as combat diving, parachuting, land warfare, as well as further individual and unit training.

During my basic training, I tried to help others who were struggling whenever I could. They assigned my cousin and me an extra task, to help the people who were failing at simple things, like learning how to make their bed properly. One guy didn't even know how to put a pillow into its case.

On runs, wearing boots and long pants, you're timed. I would be at the front and see people falling behind. I'd head back to encourage them, to motivate them to keep going. Sometimes, you had to talk rough with people, tell them that they were disappointing their mother or that their girlfriend was out dating some other guy. If I could rile them up, they'd dig in and find the energy and drive to keep going. In boot camp, I learned that if one person failed, we all failed. Teamwork was important. You need to be able to rely on the others in your unit.

We each have to realize our personal strengths and weaknesses. And, just as in the military, we all need people in our lives that we can depend on.

3

HONOR, COURAGE, COMMITMENT

*"Courage doesn't always roar. Sometimes courage is the little voice
at the end of the day that says I'll try again tomorrow."*

— *MARY ANNE RADMACHER*

EVERY RECRUIT HAS TO PASS THROUGH THE GAS EXPOSURE
chamber during boot camp. It's meant to prove to each individual that they can handle tough experiences and gain confidence in themselves and their equipment. Those short few
minutes seem to go on much longer than they really do. The
grueling training exercise is rough.

Because of my training, because I was in peak physical condition, I went in with the attitude that it might not be too bad. I
could handle it — mind over matter. I'd also been used to
offering a helping hand to those who struggled. My mask still in
place, I saw people ahead of me choking and coughing.

Inside the gas chamber, everyone stood in formation. Line by
line, recruits removed their mask. After a determined period of

time, that line of recruits left the room and the next line was instructed to remove their mask and hold it over their head. They cupped their hand below their mouth.

When they'd removed their mask, everyone's eyes teared up and burned. Their noses ran as their lungs and soft tissue rejected the CS gas. Most people choked, coughed, and struggled to breathe. Some people's knees buckled as they gagged and heaved. A few vomited into a trash can.

After watching a few rows of people remove their masks, seeing them cough and gag, watching tears run down their faces, I tried to encourage them. I said, "Hang in there, hold on."

Then, it came my turn to remove my gas mask. When I took it off, all thoughts I'd had about helping others vanished in a heartbeat. With my first inhale, it all changed; it became about personal survival.

Now, I don't want anyone to get hurt, but you have to take care of yourself first before you can help others.

When I breathed in those chemicals, I thought, "Oh, dear God." Breathing in the gas pushed me to the maximum that I could handle. The first few seconds, I realized that I was hanging on by shoestring. That string quickly became a thin strand of sewing thread.

We may have been in there for a minute, two minutes maybe, I don't know. I had tears running down my face and was coughing. Then, outside in the fresh air, I could breathe again.

Bending over, as I recovered, an eighth-grade basketball memory surfaced. The coach had us run a "monster" circuit during practice. You ran from foul line, to base line to mid-court baseline to three-quarter baseline to full-court baseline. At each point, you had to reach over and touch each line with your hand, or you failed. Then, you reversed it and ran the course backwards. Coach gave us forty-five seconds. He didn't cut us any leeway. At first, I hated him because he was so hard on us.

But later, I realized it had taught me a great deal about perseverance, about challenging myself — pushing myself as hard as I could. The times that I didn't make it within the forty-five-second time limit, I knew I'd done my best.

That early training conditioned and prepared me for the rigors of boot camp, as well as life-challenges I'd later encounter.

During SEAL training, you're constantly tested, constantly challenged. Each recruit must continually score the minimum times for each fitness test: swimming five-hundred yards, number of push-ups in two-minutes, number of sit-ups in two minutes, number of pull-ups completed, and running a mile and a half. They push you to your boundaries. If you decide to give up, signified by ringing a bell three times, you've admitted you can't continue with that schooling.

I did pass SEAL training to move onto BUD/S school. Four of us were assigned to a final test to qualify to move onto BUD/S training. My cousin didn't show up; I didn't know why at the time. Because of that, there ended up only being three of us in the timed test. It turned out my cousin didn't qualify. I was swimming and had only fifteen feet to go when a diver grabbed me and took me underwater, clear to the bottom, and held me there. It surprised me. After waiting a few seconds, I grabbed him by the knee and the ankle and pulled sharply, trying to give him a charley horse. That was the only thing I could think of to make him let go of me. He kicked me in the shoulder because I had a good hold on him. So, I released his leg and he let go of me, and we headed back up. He took me by the arm to pull me along, in case I was worn out, but I told him to let me go. I said, "I can make it on my own." I was a little riled up.

When we got up, out of the water, I was ten seconds late.

There were four men monitoring the test. I was told, "You failed, Seaman Recruit Wilson." All I could say was, "Yes, Sir."

I could have made excuses. I could have gotten mad. I could have argued that, until they took me underwater, I'd had it made. I would have passed. But, being respectful, I didn't argue.

The diver who'd taken me underwater asked why I'd grabbed his leg. I told him I'd been trying to give him a charley horse. He nodded and said, "That's what I figured."

In retrospect, I think I was being tested because I'd been at the head of the class throughout the training. They wanted to push me further and see what I could do and how I'd react.

My heart pounded so hard; it felt like it was going to beat out of my chest. Not only had I exerted myself, swimming at the top of my ability, but the diver had also unexpectedly pulled me under. Then, I realized I hadn't made the time and was told I'd failed. I did my best to stand, obey orders, and accept my failed score and to face the disappointment.

After a few long seconds of standing there in silence, one of the officers spoke. "You passed, Seaman Recruit Wilson." There were grins all around. Mine was the biggest.

I answered, "Yes, Sir. Thank you, Sir." I might have said *thank you* a few times too many. One finally said, "Get the hell out of here," but he said it with a smile.

After eight weeks of basic, the company commander had selected, out of eighty-eight people in my class, the top five people. My cousin and I were in the same training class. We were both in the top five chosen. I later learned that I was in the number one position. One of the perks of being in the top five was that, if you hadn't previously gotten a guaranteed "A" school, you then were able to choose an "A" school.

I chose military police. That way, if I didn't make it through SEAL training, I would fall back to military police school and work as an M.P. for four years, then continue with a criminal justice career after the military. When they offered me a career as Mess Specialist as my only choice of schooling, they admitted that in their time in the service, they'd never seen that happen, where the recruit's first choice, second choice, and third choice were not available. More than that, the only option available was cooking.

I had proven myself fit, willing, and ready. Yet, they were

going to start over, ignore my abilities and try to teach me to cook. That just made no sense to me. They could have just as easily tried to teach me to flap my arms and fly to the moon.

At my age and level of experience I had at the time, I was respectful. I didn't argue with their decision. Back then, I didn't know how to advocate for myself. It was an absolute that I couldn't be a cook.

They did send me to three weeks of Mess Specialist training. I finished top of the class, surprisingly. I learned about measurements and techniques. After the first week and a half, they evaluated everyone. I couldn't go to BUD/S training, so I relented and attended Mess Specialist. Basically, to buy time. I really wanted either submarine school, which was hard to get into, or SEALS training.

Alan Monohan, a U.S. Representative for West Virginia's first congressional district, came to my aid. The Navy invited me to return to San Diego and continue training. At that point, they said I could go into BUD/S training — which had been my goal all along.

However, once my trust had been broken, my spirit had been broken. I felt I couldn't believe they'd uphold the promise they were making. Were they setting me up? Would I wind up as a Mess Specialist if I went back to San Diego? The availability for BUD/S training had been off the table only a few weeks earlier. They'd sent eighty-eight recruits through SEALS training when, according to the Navy, there were no SEALS openings.

It was a difficult decision. I chose not to return. Part of me still regrets not taking the chance. It was a painful time in my life. Those memories still bother me, but I can't dwell on that time; I'm at a different place in my life now.

This story, about my athleticism, my abilities, and how I survived and came out number one in my Navy SEALS school, wasn't written to brag. I don't mean to boast or make myself look better than anyone.

This story has been shared only to show how far I'd fallen in the space of a few months from a fit, lean, athletic young man to the same lean young man in a wheelchair.

4

DREAMS SHATTERED, GOALS ANNIHILATED

"Getting over a painful experience is much like crossing monkey bars. You have to let go at some point in order to move forward."

— *C.S. LEWIS*

BACK IN WEST VIRGINIA, I HAD TO COME TO TERMS WITH MY separation from the U.S. Navy. I had to absorb the overwhelming feelings of being isolated, defeated, and broken-hearted. My spirit had been crushed. I'd given everything I had to give. Throughout boot camp and training, I'd remained at the top of my classes, and I'd passed SEAL school then ended up in the number one position. I'd also passed a background check for a government security clearance.

Obtaining a discharge from the Navy isn't something that can be done quickly. It took a couple of months of back and forth corresponding with them before I was, eventually, discharged. So, that delay carried and kept alive the negative emotions that fed on me daily. While they'd offered me a chance to come back to San Diego, finish three more weeks of training and then offer me a place in BUD/S program, I couldn't do it. My trust in them was gone. After they'd broken their promise one too many times, I lost faith and knew in my heart that if I went back, I'd end up as a Mess Specialist, learning how to cook.

In the ensuing months, I found a job, a few jobs, to pay the bills and not depend on my parents. It was easy to fall back into my old job of mowing lawns; to that, I added landscaping to my services offered to our faithful clients, many of whom had been with us for years.

To fill the too-many leftover hours in the day, I began going out with friends. Sometimes to a bar. Then, more often than not, almost always to a bar. Drinking became the escape from the misery my life had become. Over the next few months, it increased in frequency and became my number one pastime.

I dated a few girls but always gave them a disclaimer upfront, "If you're looking for a friend, someone to hang out with, have dinner or go to a movie together, that's great. But if you're looking for a romantic relationship, I'm not your man."

My life was in near-complete disconnect. My emotions were raw. Losing my dream of becoming a SEAL was more than I could bear. My personality is, *I don't give up*. But, even with everything I'd done right with the Navy, it still felt like I'd had a rug pulled out from under me. I'd given them 100%. There had been so much potential – I was right for that career. Then, they'd informed me there was a major roadblock to my dream.

My life had hit a brick wall, and with nowhere to turn, I turned to alcohol to numb the pain.

When people reach a point of loneliness and despair, and they have nowhere to go, there's not even a fork in the road, there's not even a road, they hit rock bottom. That's what I did.

I still worked. Car sales kept me going for a while.

Even though it hadn't been diagnosed, I realize now that I had clinical depression, if not PTSD. It was that traumatic for me. I am a perfectionist. As I said, I don't accept failure, and I keep trying until I succeed.

But at the end of the workday, there I'd be, at a bar.

Again.

I went to work just enough to get a paycheck, enough to cover any expenses necessary for survival. I didn't own up to being responsible; I didn't enroll in college. I didn't put partying to the side. My lifestyle was fixed in the short term. Any long-term goals couldn't be considered. I had no passion; the vision was gone. Also, I had noticed that ex-servicemen had difficulty in reintegrating themselves when going back to civilian life. I hadn't been in the military all that long, nor had I seen active duty, but I had pinned all my hopes and dreams on that goal, so I felt displaced when working in my hometown, doing civilian jobs.

Basketball was always the one place where I could go to get things off my mind. I did occasionally play a pickup game. I'd always been a highly competitive person. Maybe that's why I took the loss of becoming a SEAL so hard. It felt like a defeat.

During this period of a few months, I continually lived at a breaking point. There was no way to prepare for a setback of this magnitude. Life had thrown me a major curveball when I'd had my life all mapped out. I planned on being a SEAL for the rest of my Navy career. It was even hard for me to identify that I wasn't the same person as I'd been before SEAL school.

Until the accident, I didn't understand that I possessed skills that I could have used to make something of myself, other than being a Navy SEAL or working in the government. While I did need a college degree for the goal of working with the FBI or DEA, I realized later that nobody needs a college degree just to go get a job.

But I was a twenty-year-old adrenaline junkie who had big dreams. I was that guy you'd see on the tallest, fastest, steepest rollercoaster, screaming, "Faster!" while wearing a grin as wide as the sky.

So, I turned, more and more often, to drinking.

However, turning to alcohol to be the salve for your wounds won't actually fix anything in the long run. It can only ever be a very temporary relief.

The website, TheJournal.ie, explains in an article, 1"Alcohol Hurts Your Mental Health," why you may not realize that alcohol could be impacting your mental health:

People tend to drink more when experiencing moderate to high levels of shyness or fear, and those who suffer from anxiety can be tempted to use alcohol to help cope with it. Initially, you may feel like it provides relief to some symptoms as it depresses the central nervous system, but it can worsen these symptoms in the long-run.

Drinking to relieve stress can in the long-term worsen that stress, intensifying anxiety and irritability after drinking. As it leaves the body, alcohol's effects on brain chemistry can cause the symptoms of anxiety and panic attacks, even in people who never suffered anxiety.

Similar to its impact on anxiety, not only can alcohol worsen depression, it can actually cause it too. When the effects of alcohol wear off, it changes our brain chemistry for the worse. In fact, people who drink heavily are more likely to suffer from depression, and alcohol dependence is roughly three times more likely among people with depression.

A good night's sleep restores our body and minds and is vital to minding your mental health. Because alcohol is a depressant it makes you sleepy at times but the sleep you get after drinking is of a much lower quality than the sleep you get when you are not drinking.

This is because alcohol can reduce the amount of Rapid Eye Movement (REM) sleep you get, leaving you feeling drowsy, low in energy and you may find it harder to concentrate the next day.

IT STOPS YOU FROM DEVELOPING HEALTHY COPING MECHANISMS.

It is worthwhile to learn healthy coping mechanisms in response to emotions like stress, sadness, and anger that do not involve or rely on alcohol. One of the most effective ways of doing this is to get the right support for your individual needs. In fact, a study by the HSE into alcohol-related harm found that, "those who were engaged in regular heavy drinking were less likely to use positive coping strategies when dealing with anxiety and depression."

If a person repeatedly turns to alcohol when their mood deteriorates, they miss out on the opportunity of discovering other, more effective, ways of dealing with unpleasant moods. Learning new ways to cope can make us stronger, healthier, and happier in the long term.

Their sub-heading is important to point out, "Drink Less and You'll Be Better Able to Cope with Everyday Stresses." When you're craving a drink to take the edge off your anxiety/stress/fear, remember that alcohol isn't a good solution.

I hope you noticed that bold-faced sentence in the middle of the article. "It (alcohol) stops you from developing healthy coping mechanisms." It's an important lesson to understand. I had to learn — the hard way — how to develop coping mechanisms. Later in the book, we'll cover the use of tools that will help you realize a problem or a trigger is heading your way and how to take measures to prevent the situation from worsening.

On my way to the bar, I'd think about how I needed to enroll in West Virginia State College. But somehow, I never got around to actually doing it. My backup goal in life was to continue with earning a degree in criminology. I still had that desire to work for the FBI or the DEA.

At the time, though, my psyche was too beat up to make any constructive steps in my life. I needed time to recover from having those dreams of becoming a Navy SEAL ripped from my grasp. To compound that problem, I knew those government agencies only accepted top-notch people. I wasn't in a good mental state to start taking courses, much less excel in my studies.

So, all along the way, I didn't use any coping skills, wellness tools, action plans, or trigger shutdowns. At that point, I didn't have any of those tools in my mental arsenal.

If you find yourself in a similar situation, whatever the cause, please read this entire book. I want you to have ways to avoid walking into mental land mines, to learn how to lessen the stress on your mental state and emotional being. I want you to have wellness tools to live a better, happier life.

5

A MOMENT IN TIME

"Everyone has a thousand wishes before a tragedy, but just one afterward."

— *FREDRIK BACKMAN, AUTHOR OF*
BEARTOWN

THAT MORNING BEGAN LIKE ANY OTHER. I WENT TO WORK ON the 2:00 to 8:00 pm shift, selling cars. Of course, it wasn't my dream job. I'd planned on finishing up with BUD/S school right about that time. I was supposed to be a SEAL, not selling cars. But it paid the bills, so I had no choice. I still had a slight connection with the Navy. When I ran across a fit, young person who met the criteria, I'd give them a card from a Navy recruiter.

My attitude wasn't good. I was sending candidates to the Navy – where I should have been. Mentally and emotionally, I wasn't in a good place. Life had gone all topsy-turvy — just when I had planned my future, worked for it, and had been so close to achieving my goal, it disappeared like water vapor under a hot sun.

The day was a Thursday. August 28, 1992. When I got off work, the sun was hanging low on the horizon, gifting us with the last of its light for the day. Most workdays, a couple of buddies and I went to hit the gym and work out.

Older than J.T. and me, Jimmy was a bodybuilder; he'd won the title of Mr. West Virginian, and he'd earned it. The three of us worked at the car lot, so we had an established routine for working out. I wasn't looking to build the type of muscles Jimmy had; I just wanted to maintain my muscle tone and stay in shape. I had a body fat of 4% and, with the amount of drinking I was doing, I also needed to work out to burn off those calories.

We finished up at the gym about 10:00 pm and dropped Jimmy off at home. J.T. was a groundskeeper for some wealthy people. They were away at the time, and J.T. had full use of their home and car collection.

We were driving a Nissan 300ZX, borrowed from J.T.'s employers. Being the thinnest, I had been squeezed in the back, where there was no seat, just a bit of space. I rode like that from the dealership to the gym, about ten minutes.

The two-seater "Z" cars were fast sports cars. This one featured a T-top. The roof of the car had removable glass panels, one on each side. A metal bar ran between them, offering support for the glass inserts. However, that narrow metal bar also provided the only structural integrity for the roof.

J.T. and I headed to a bar for a buddy's birthday party; it was "Drink or Drown" night. We got there about 11:00 pm and drank a couple of beers each. J.T.'s girlfriend was there – she was an airline stewardess. I danced with several women. I'm not shy.

One night, there was a circle of seven women dancing by themselves. So, I took myself to the dance floor to join them. The possibility of rejection didn't bother me, either they'd dance with me or tell me to get lost. At that point in my life, I was just looking for a good time; it was my mindset. I was still reeling from what had happened with the military. The only serious girlfriend I'd had, ended up cheating on me a year or so before, during spring break. I hadn't gotten over that, either. The hurt ran deep from both experiences; they both felt like a betrayal.

Around midnight, we left the bar. Neither of us had drank too much; we'd just sat, danced or talked while sipping our beer. Back in the "Z" car, J.T. was, of course, driving. After all, it was his (borrowed) car.

We hit a four-lane highway, heading to that huge, gorgeous house I called a mansion. J.T.'s girlfriend and another girl were driving there separately. A thirty-minute drive away was a twenty-five-year-old beautiful woman waiting for me. It was a good night.

J.T. usually drove a bit fast. This particular night, driving that Nissan 300ZX, he drove faster than usual. I admit some anticipation, so it wasn't until I saw a sign that said, "Dunbar," that I glanced over at the dashboard and noticed we were traveling at 125 mph.

"Whoa, maybe you should slow down a bit," I said.

He did — a bit.

Driving in the left lane, we approached a vehicle driving in the right lane. I think, because of our how fast we came upon them, they hadn't seen us. The car began moving to the left lane — the lane we occupied. Obviously, J.T. had intended to fly past them. We were going much faster than they were. The other driver saw us at the last minute and swerved.

J.T. swerved, too. Unfortunately, both cars veered from the left lane to the right lane.

After J.T. swung into the right lane, I knew we'd probably hit the other car. Maybe he jerked the wheel into the berm and slammed on the brakes. Maybe the momentum was too much for the car.

As I saw the accident unfolding, I had the time to think, "Oh, shit, this is gonna hurt." But I figured we'd just bounce off the guardrail and smash up the car.

There was no guardrail where we went off the road.

I don't know how it happened — but the car rolled.

The other car kept driving, I learned later. I don't know how many times we rolled. With the inertia, it could have been quite a few times. The car settled, upside-down, in a culvert, at 12:30 at night.

God is our refuge and strength, A very present help in trouble.
Therefore we will not fear, though the earth should change
  And though the mountains slip into the heart of the sea;
Though its waters roar and foam,
  Though the mountains quake at its swelling pride.
  Selah.

— *PSALM 46:1-3 NASB*

AFTER A FEW MOMENTS, we both realized that we'd stopped moving.

"You okay, Mike?" J.T. asked.

I was hanging upside-down, trapped by the seat belt. At the time, I didn't realize the car was resting on its roof. I was pretty dazed.

I said, "Yes, I'm okay, but I can't feel my legs." My eyes were closed, but I felt broken glass on my face. I couldn't raise my hands to wipe it off. They didn't work. I knew something was wrong, but I couldn't figure it out.

J.T. had glass pieces on him. He managed to climb out of the car.

It was about a week and a half later that I found out we'd flipped and landed twenty-five feet from the road in the culvert.

I hung there, unable to move or even open my eyes because of the glass. I felt damp. After a long while, I heard sirens.

The medics arrived. I heard them talking. Someone asked me how I was doing.

"I'm okay. Just get me out of here." A few moments went by. I might have passed out. Memories of that time are intermittent at best. The next time someone talked to me, I said, "I can't feel my legs, but I'll be okay if you can just get me out of here."

Time seemed to crawl. When I was aware of my surroundings, I got hit with anxiety. I wanted out of that car like nothing I'd ever wanted before. It felt like it had been forty-five minutes I'd hung there after the wreck.

The firemen said they were going to have to use some lifting airbags to raise the car in order to get me out. Everything was a slow and careful process. The firemen have to be careful not to further injure victims, but they also have to protect themselves. I heard bits and pieces of what people around me were saying. They pumped the car up, inch by inch. Then, one of the lifting bags broke. They needed two to raise the car up enough because the car was lying in the culvert.

I heard a man yell. "You need some help?"

He was a salesman who sold equipment to fire departments. As if by some miracle, he was driving the same road, late at night, and had samples in his car. The firemen asked if he had any lifting airbags.

"Yes. I have two," he hollered back.

I started having trouble breathing. My arms were weak. All I could do was lay there, helplessly, fighting panic, while waiting for rescue. Finally, they were able to lift the car enough. I was near hysterical, feeling so trapped, like a tree had fallen on me.

I told the fireman, "Please... just get me out of this car." I knew that if I could get out, I could regain feeling in my legs, shake off the soreness and straighten out the kinks from being cramped up. I'd be fine. Give me two hours, I'll recover.

Then, after waiting for the car to be pumped up, I was told

that they were going to have to use the Jaws of Life on the car to extricate me. I was fighting to breathe, starting to blackout, praying when I was lucid. *Please let me hang on, God.*

The fireman told me he had to put a towel around me, so when he cut into the T-top bar, nothing would fall on me.

I was on the verge of totally losing it. I had to push my mental strength past any limitations. I remembered back to my athletic and military training... *push past that point, beyond where you thought you could go.*

As I learned much later, the T-top bar had smashed when the car rolled. I happened to be in the wrong place at the instant it collapsed. It pushed my chin down to my chest and my face was over my shoulder.

After he finished cutting the metal, they started to pull me out. The next thing I knew, I was in an ambulance. Things were fuzzy. I guess they inserted an IV, or gave me oxygen. Or both. They did what they had to. I did what I had to, which was trying to stay alert and focus on breathing.

A few minutes later, I heard a helicopter. It was a medical emergency helicopter. That was my first inkling that the situation was far worse than I thought.

I knew they were coming for me.

REALITY

"For I am the Lord your God, who upholds your right hand, Who says to you, 'Do not fear, I will help you.'"

— *ISAIAH 41:13*

THE HELICOPTER LANDED IN SHAWNEE PARK, A MILE AND A half down the road from the crash. The ambulance transported me to it. I don't remember much; I fought to stay conscious. They'd inserted an IV to keep me stable... well, it had somehow appeared there. I hadn't noticed.

When we took off, I realized we were in the air. The medical staff were talking to me, but I had no idea what they were saying. Five minutes later, we landed on the roof of the hospital. As I tried to stay awake, I was aware they were carrying me and running.

In the E.R., they did a whole bunch of stuff to keep me alive.

I don't know what all they did... steroids for inflammation. My head had been strapped down so I couldn't move.

In a room with a whole team of people, one woman asked me, "Who should we call?"

"Call my mom," I croaked out and gave her the phone number. "Tell her I'm in trouble, but I'm all right." Yeah, that sounds like crazy talk, but I was a mess.

My mother worked at an office with orthopedic surgeons. She knew about medicine and would understand medical jargon.

They ran some tests... or maybe a hundred tests.

I was glad when Mom and Dad got there. Their familiar faces reassured me. But then I realized that their faces showed fear. It was hard to think, going in and out of consciousness. A doctor came in and used a needle to poke me in several places, asking if I could feel it. He was looking for a feeling of sensation in my legs, torso, and arms.

I answered, "Yes... no... yes," each time he asked if I could feel the pinprick. But really, they were all a "No." I couldn't feel anything. The reality of having zero feeling in any part of my legs was too difficult to accept.

The next thing I knew, I was on my way to the X-ray area. The X-ray technician was a young, attractive woman. Something I'll never forget was when she was putting the X-ray plates under my neck, and I caught a look on her face. Her eyes told me everything. That got to me. She'd just confirmed my worst nightmare, the thoughts I'd been trying to keep out of my head. The fear threatened to suffocate me. I knew I was in trouble — big trouble.

I had to redirect my thoughts. The young lady was very attractive and about my age. As I lay there, in my mind, I visually appreciated her for her pretty face and that she had become an X-ray tech at such a young age. Still trying to keep the fear at bay, I thought, "I should not be lying here. I should be on a date..." I glanced at her face and finished my thought. "With her."

Keep positive — that was the thought that kept me going. I said something to her, to try and relax my tension. I don't remember what I said; it was an attempt at humor. I wasn't there long. They soon took me back to the E.R.

Something for pain was injected into my I.V. Next thing I knew, I was in the I.C.U. I'd been in a procedure, and my head was in traction. Screws had been inserted in my forehead all around to the back. They had been drilled into my skull to hold a halo crown. The halo is done to relieve pressure from the injured area and to immobilize the patient. *Me.* I'd never been immobile in my life, now I couldn't turn my head even a few degrees. That thing hurt. I tried not to think about it, instead asked my mom what time she'd be coming back in the morning.

"What time do you want us back here?"

"Six o'clock," I answered. It was probably already 3:00 a.m. at that point.

The nurse said, "You gotta give your parents more time than that."

But I didn't want to be there alone. I was so overwhelmed with fear to the point it crippled me.

"I'll be with you, all night long. I promise," the nurse said.

"Okay," I answered.

While that was great, a nurse wasn't the same as having my mom there. I knew she'd been holding her emotions in check — probably for my sake. Most likely she'd broken down and cried while I was gone for X-rays. Selfishly, I still didn't want Mom to go and leave me alone with reality.

The next morning, a few doctors came in and explained the surgery I'd need. Mom's boss was one of the doctors. There was also a neurologist in my room and, I think, a nephrologist. I'd broken no bones — which was a miracle — except my neck. The C6 and C7, the sixth and seventh cervical vertebrae were broken.

The doctor planned a procedure to insert a metal rod and a plate between C5 and C7 to stabilize my neck.

The next thing to wonder about was when the surgery would be. As it turned out, not soon.

Every day, the doctor kept saying, "One more day." The next day, it was the same thing. "One more day."

The halo crown had to stay on until surgery. It took six days before they performed the surgery. I didn't leave that room for six days.

Only my family was allowed into the I.C.U. to visit. The nurse would come and tell me who was in the waiting room. Even though they couldn't come into my room, they still came. My dad went to talk to those in the waiting room, to pass on information and tell them we appreciated their visit.

To one woman, he said, "Oh, you must be April." April was a girl I'd dated.

She shook her head. "No, I'm Tiffany."

He came back to my room and told me what happened. He was embarrassed.

"Oh, Dad, from now on, let them tell you their names. Who knows how many women will come in here?" We had a good laugh over that.

My grandparents arrived from Cleveland. I'd never seen my grandpa cry. As soon as he walked into my room, he broke down in tears.

"I'll be okay, Grandpa." I tried to reassure him. "Once they get surgery done, I'll be okay."

However, when everyone left for the day, I was alone with my thoughts. Despair, loneliness, and guilt took over. I felt that I should have prevented the accident. I should have made him slow down. *Who's going to want me now? I'm paralyzed... nobody is going to want me.* The tears ran freely down my cheeks.

Nights were the most painful part. I was still hopeful about regaining some movement, and I knew I'd walk differently, but confident I'd at least be able to walk. I just did not want to be paralyzed in a wheelchair. Even though I'd been a jock, I'd always considered myself a nice guy. Each year I'd kept my focus on sports.

I hadn't even had a serious girlfriend until my senior year.

I thought about my family and what they were going through. My friends... how would I fit into the same life? Where was my life going now? I had to forget about the military and college. If I'm not able to walk, what's that going to be like? The fear of the unknown was a powerful enemy.

Then, trying to accept the inevitable, I wondered, *How is my life going to change? Can I recover?* Back to denial. I can beat this. I've trained my body. I can do it.

After they inserted the rods and the crown came off, the doctor came in to discuss my outlook. After the surgery, I'd been moved to the trauma floor.

He said, "You have about a 2% chance of walking again, ever, in your life. Unless a miracle happens."

Self-pity overtook me. I tried to have faith. My only source of comfort was calling on God and a Bible verse.

And we know that God causes all things to work together for good to those who love God, to those who are called according to His purpose.

— *ROMANS 8:28*

I HUNG onto that verse with every bit of strength I had left.

I never found out who called to report the accident. Most people didn't have cell phones back then. Only rich or important people had "bag phones" that stayed in the car. It might have been someone with a phone. There also were houses not too far from where we crashed. Somebody might have heard the accident and called.

One day, a man named Bill went into the orthopedic office where my mom worked. He was a patient with a knee issue. He discovered her name and asked if I was her son.

"Why, yes," she said.

"I was at the scene of your son's accident. I'll tell you this, never in my twenty-five years of being a fireman had I ever seen such a mess as that wreck. Your son should not be alive now, with the shape that car was in. It was on top of him, and with that T-top bar pinning his neck to his chest and his chin to his shoulder..." He paused to shake his head. "Only by the grace of God that boy is alive."

Bill came by two or three days after that to visit me. He told me that by the time they'd gotten me out of the car, I'd blacked out. So, of course, I didn't remember him.

He said, "After that lifting airbag broke, there's no way we could've gotten you out. Then there was that salesman, *who just happened to be driving by...* well after midnight. A guy who sells lifting airbags of all things. He made the choice to stop and see if he could help. Was it by chance he had some airbags with him? That was the one piece of equipment we needed to save your life." He took a deep breath and exhaled slowly. "Was all that only a coincidence? I don't think so." He looked at me, straight in the eyes. "From where you lay in that bed, it may not seem like it right now. But I'll tell you the honest truth... God is watching over you."

AFTERMATH

"Obstacles don't have to stop you. If you run into a wall, don't turn around and give up. Figure out how to climb it, go through it, or work around it."

— *MICHAEL JORDAN*

AFTER I'D STABILIZED ENOUGH FROM THE ACCIDENT AND THEN the surgery, they sent me to the Shepherd Center in Atlanta by helicopter medevac. Among other critical health issues, the center specializes in spinal cord injury rehabilitation. Treating a patient with a spinal cord injury isn't just about caring for the site itself. The whole body has been affected and must be handled by knowledgeable professionals.

At this point, I was still living with a certain level of denial. I'd convinced myself that if they could get me to a rehab specialist, I'd pull through. I had spent my whole life pushing my body for that extra mile, pushing my willpower and my mind to overcome fatigue and stress. I could do it. *I could walk again.*

The first thing the center had to do was assess me to determine if I was a good candidate for their program. My parents and I stayed in a nearby hotel. Within a few days, we got a call that I'd been accepted. I arrived on October 26th and was discharged on December 18th.

My twenty-first birthday was *celebrated* at the Shepherd Center.

There were noticeable differences between the two facilities. When I was in the hospital in West Virginia, they set up a program for several therapies at various intervals throughout the day. When you didn't have therapy, physical or otherwise, you stayed in the hospital bed.

In Atlanta, they got you up at 7:30 a.m., whether you had anything scheduled or not. In West Virginia, they brought you breakfast to your room. In Atlanta, every day, it was "Get out of bed." They took you to breakfast instead of bringing meals to the patient's room. Aides would get us out of bed and into a manual wheelchair, then push us down the hall to the dining area.

Facing the task of feeding myself, there were new hurdles. Like, how do I open my milk carton? The other quadriplegics and I had to figure that one out. We used our teeth to pry the carton open. We even had races to see who could be the first to open the milk.

Shepherd's goal was to teach us how to manage everyday tasks on our own and re-integrate us into our homes. So, every day, we were sent to classes, physical therapy or occupational therapy. We had classes to learn about our body — the same body we'd been living with but now needed alternative ways to manage the body's functions.

In one class, they were trying to get me to put on my pants, they were pull-up pants, specially adapted with loops sewn into the waistband. I was getting really frustrated, giving it everything I had, and trying to comply with what they told me to do. I was smart — but having no dexterity in my fingers made it nearly impossible. Mom could see that my frustration was building, I wasn't taking it out on medical people, but was about ready to blow a gasket. Mom told the occupation therapy person, "You're pushing him, he's worked up now, but I promise you this. He will never leave the house without his pants on."

I love my mom.

She got a small apartment just across the street, on Peachtree Road, so she could walk over and attend some of the classes with me. Other patients had spouses or parents there to help understand the methods we had to use to function in daily life. It wasn't fun by any means, but it was necessary since our bodies no longer had the muscle control to handle ordinary activities like emptying our bowels. Paralysis disrupts the bowel system; since voluntary control of the external anal sphincter is affected, it must be accomplished by other means.

So, at night, there was a bowel program where we, along with our caregivers (spouse, parent) learned how to properly execute digital manipulation to stimulate evacuation.

My parents and I lived in a rural area in West Virginia where home health care was unavailable or of poor quality, so my dear mother was left to fill the void. She eventually quit her job to care for me. It was considerably awkward for both of us, but necessary. After some time, I converted to another method that didn't require daily manual manipulation to empty my gut.

That is just one example of how difficult life can become when you've lost control of the muscles in your legs and, many times, your arms as well.

While at Shepherd, I had time between classes, so I could wander the halls. With doors open, I saw people in far worse condition than myself. Sometimes, people had a trach tube in their throat.

Depending on where, in the spinal cord, a person's injury took place, they might retain full use of their arms, or they might require prolonged mechanical ventilation due to respiratory insufficiency. In other words, a machine breathes for them via a hose down their throat.

Occasionally, I'd see a young person, a child. There were twelve, thirteen, and fourteen-year-old kids there. It was more than I could bear to see them, think of them, barely having begun life — and now facing the rest of it living in a wheelchair.

The Shepherd facility kept us busy, so we didn't have time to dwell on our situations. And, by that time, my emotions weren't quite as raw as immediately following the accident. Unless you had a medical reason, you didn't spend your day in bed. We could go to recreational therapy. We could shoot pool with adapted pool sticks. There was a gym and a *swimming* pool — well, it was water therapy.

After dinner, it was back to bed.

When I had sufficiently adapted and learned enough, I was sent home. Then, reality set in. I was back in my same pre-accident bedroom. Only I had changed drastically. Everything had to be adapted to fit my new needs... stairs, the bathroom, furniture rearranged in my bedroom. Wheelchairs take up a good amount of room. They also have to fit through doorways.

In the beginning, I only got out of the house for doctor appointments. Buddies came by to visit. While I was learning how to put on clothes, they'd moved on with their goals. They had gone to college or even gotten married. They were *doing* things. I was busy trying to move my legs regularly to prevent blood clots, caring for my skin to avoid pressure sores, maintaining proper blood pressure and many more irregularities you have to be concerned with when you've become paralyzed.

I had to get a grip. Depression is a normal occurrence after a life-changing accident. I was dealing with anger, resentment, heartache, and the ever-present denial about my situation. I wondered, *Will I ever have a girlfriend again?* I'd gone from a fairly good-looking twenty-year-old to a fairly good-looking but been-through-hell twenty-one-year-old, now in a wheelchair instead of running up and down a basketball court.

Part of me realized I had to snap out of it, and not focus too much on the negative potential of my future life, or it would eat me up with bitterness. The accident had happened on August 28, 1992. Early in 1993, I was mostly stuck at home. Since she no longer worked, my mom watched TV occasionally. But the one routine every day was at 3:00 pm. Oprah appeared in my living room. Topics for discussion included: "Women whose friends and family don't want them to reconcile with the man in their lives." Or, "Suspicious Wives go Overboard."

After a daily diet of this, I knew I had to get out of the house. I couldn't handle much more of that kind of topic, discussed *ad nauseam* for an hour. I'm sure America loved Oprah, but for me, someone who'd been headed for a life as a Navy SEAL, it wasn't my choice of programming. However, it was winter and that complicated getting out of the house.

I don't want to say that Oprah drove me to better myself, but the TV show certainly was a catalyst.

When faced with a difficult task, giving up is the easy way out. Making something of yourself is hard. But, you are the only person who can help yourself. There are things which *only you* have control over. And there are times in life that you aren't able to change anything — except your attitude. If you have goals, dreams, and they inspire you, you have to figure out how to achieve them despite all the roadblocks in your path.

I learned how to accept personal responsibility. I realized that, if life doesn't change — and it probably won't — then I'm just treading water. A person can only do that for so long. They're not moving forward. They're stagnating. Or giving up. I had to adapt and learn and grow.

Michael Jordan had always been a hero to me. He was a phenomenal basketball player, possessing the ability to push himself on the court as well as the gym. His exercise routine became famous.

At this point in my life, I needed inspiration — and Michael Jordan provided it. He played with the Bulls and was a world-class athlete. Widely regarded as the NBA's greatest all-time player, Michael Jordan won six titles during his time with the Chicago Bulls.

Taking a cue from my past and from Michael, I had to push myself. If I needed to exercise my upper body strength, I told myself I'd do five minutes. Next time, I'd do seven minutes. I had to train my body, but also my mind. I had to learn how to process and handle the emotions that threatened my goals. Negative feelings continually lived near the surface. I learned to refocus my feelings, desires, frustrations, and goals. I had to target my objectives, reexamine, reevaluate my situation, and set in place a plan of action.

Michael Jordan taught me about confidence, how to create a foundation, then build on it. I learned how to put the pieces together to overcome obstacles. Recalling time both spent in sports, as well as my military training, taught me how to grow as a team, where, together, everyone achieves more. At that point, I was my own team.

It took me about two years to begin to drive again. I had to get up a ramp into the van and transfer to a swiveling driver's seat. The transfer from wheelchair to driver's seat took twenty minutes. It was exhausting. I'd drive five miles and then be completely worn out. As time went by, I built up my stamina to drive more than five miles. But I also experienced setbacks — more denial stages. At one point, I decided that I wasn't going to drive if this was what it took. *Forget it. I'll get somebody to drive me around.*

One day, a friend was driving my van. Without warning, he pulled over and said, "You're driving."

"No, I'm not." He insisted.

I told him, "I'm used to sitting. I'll sit here for an hour. *Whatever.* Not driving." After fifteen minutes of a stalemate, I gave in.

After that, I began driving again. I built up my coordination and upper body strength, so it took less time to move to the driver's seat. I eventually got to the point I could transfer in only three minutes, swivel around and be ready to go.

Now, I have a power chair and don't have to transfer. My current van is set up so I drive from my wheelchair. The chair fits into the van, using an easy-lock system. Several 3/4" bolts hold my power chair securely. I see people at clinics now, and think, *It's really tough getting in and out of non-adaptive van.*

Over the course of time, and with a good amount of pushing, I eventually gained a little more confidence in myself. Now, I drive all over, go to physical therapy, out to lunch, and a few functions.

I've had speaking engagements; my desire is to help others. In 2011, I was at the National Council for Independent Living in Washington, D.C. We had lunch by the Washington Monument. A few senators came and spoke. I was fortunate to sit near them. We had a round-table discussion regarding improvements for the disabled community. By 2013, I was asked to speak at a huge disability awareness event in the West Virginia capital of Charleston, where I continue to serve on the board of the West Virginia Appalachian Center for Independent Living.

If you don't have confidence, you won't be successful, whatever your goals are. You have to stay true to your goal. Ask yourself, why are you here? Are you a leader? A speaker?

Don't be an armchair quarterback. Get in the game.

Be involved. Be intuitive, take the initiative.

Run with it.

8

PERSEVERANCE

"I can do all things through Christ, who strengthens me."

— *PHILIPPIANS 4:13*

In 1998, about six years after the accident, I purchased a used car lot in West Virginia. It was small, but I managed to keep a few employees. My cousin worked there and helped me with the day-to-day operations.

Applying myself at the car lot gave me peace of mind. Just to be working again made me feel like I was an important, contributing part of the community. It helped me psychologically, physically, and emotionally. I felt better in so many ways because I was no longer spending my days at home, just hanging out. I'd already lost too many hours of my life watching TV. And way too many hours of watching Oprah.

Going to the car lot got me out of the house Monday through Saturday. I worked fifty-five to sixty hours a week —

usually 9:00 am to closing, which was 6:00 pm. In the summertime, we usually wouldn't get out until around 7:00 or when the sun went down.

After the tragedy of September 11, 2001, the economy suffered. The U.S. had already been struggling through a moderate recession. The terrorist attacks of 9/11 affected Americans so strongly that it further impaired businesses that were already fighting to stay afloat. In 2003, the first signs of the housing crisis were noticed; Warren Buffet wrote to his shareholders warning them of latent, but potentially lethal danger.

I decided it was a good time to sell the car lot – I'd had it for about five years. After that, I tried to go back to college and finish my degree. It didn't work out. It didn't take long to find out that being around people my age in the college environment was difficult. I felt uneasy — insignificant — there. The environment, with so many capable, smart people, caused me to become overly emotional. Social anxiety built inside me. Time spent on the campus left me with no positive outlook for the future. So, as hard as it was to leave, it was harder still to stay.

I became an employee for a small chain of furniture stores. My specialty was in the bedding department. At that time, mattresses were evolving. Special training was needed to be able to help customers choose from many new materials. Since people don't buy new beds frequently, they were new to choices such as Tempur-Pedic memory foam, pillowtop mattresses, and high-tech adjustable sleep sets. Bedding manufacturers also realized an opportunity existed to cater to people with medical issues. So, I became a bedding specialist for a company with stores in West Virginia, Ohio, and Kentucky.

Since the construction of beds had changed, furniture sales associates didn't have the proper knowledge to handle customer questions. I enjoyed working there. My shifts were usually Tuesday through Thursday from 11:00 to 9:00, Saturday 11:00 to 6:00, and some Sundays as needed. It was a forty-plus hour a week job, however, early in the week, only a few people would shop for beds. Since I was working on commission, I had to learn to adjust. I also had to learn how to handle many hours without customers — boredom set in quite often.

I met a woman while working there; she was also an employee. We dated for a while. Then, in 2006, I took a leave of absence and headed to Florida.

My Chrysler van had a heated driver's seat. It also had a defect in the heating element below the upholstery. It overheated and caught on fire. Since I have no feeling in my buttocks, I was unaware of the tissue damage that occurred while I was driving.

I had treatment for the three lesions caused by the seat, but there was a lot of friction on my skin, so nothing could be done to help me heal.

Later, I went to Key West. I'd thought the leather upholstery on the seat was breaking down, so I had a guy look at the seats. He called and told me that the van seat heater had caught on fire and scorched through the foam to the leather seat. This was the first I'd known of the seat heater causing my injuries.

I tried to go back to work for a while, but my skin had been so compromised that, no matter how weight shifts I did, it didn't help. Weight shifts are when you lean from side to side to briefly relieve pressure from each side of the buttocks.

Chrysler had a defect in their vans — the seat heaters. All the vans they made had this problem — not just the ones modified for disabled drivers. They never issued a recall, despite many people having problems with seats overheating and causing injury. There are consumer complaints on the internet dating as late as 2015 as a failure date on a 2014 Chrysler Town & Country. Many purchasers have complained about seats overheating, usually in localized spots. Sometimes, a hole would be burned through the upholstery.

I suffered from sustained open wounds and, eventually, had to have five surgeries — which caused me to be unemployed. I did contact an attorney and pursued a lawsuit. The attorney brought in a medical expert who was a specialist in vans to testify about the defect.

After the burns, I couldn't maintain my weight. I'd stayed at 115 pounds for sixteen years after the car accident. I had virtually no body fat. Back in the hospital, the medical staff tried to keep my nutrition levels up enough for me to be adequately healthy so I could have surgery on the burn wounds. That attempt was unsuccessful. I was told to go home and try some topical medication. They didn't refer me to a specialist like Mayo clinic, or the Cleveland Clinic. It felt like, "Here's some cream for those burns, good luck." No second or third opinions were given.

Over time, I dropped from 115 pounds to 87 pounds from the burns. I was given a feeding tube — that didn't help. All the food energy I took in was being used to try and help my body heal.

I'd lost so much muscle. I couldn't change my circumstances. The medical community couldn't do anything. I laid in bed and cried. I prayed to God to help me. Then, I prayed, "God, take me home."

Tired of living like that, I took matters into my own hands. Instead of giving up, instead of waiting for a referral, I contacted the Cleveland Clinic. They got me in for an appointment right away. Maybe that was how

God answered my prayers. I took personal responsibility for myself. My choices were to give up and suffer or be proactive and take control of my health. There is a sheer inner will that triggers the body to overcome any obstacle that lies in a person's path. Be an overcomer. Draw on that inner will. I had nothing left.

You have to take charge of your own health if you've gone as far as your current doctor can take you. I had superior mesenteric artery symptoms. Along with spinal cord injuries, it requires a specialist even for regular care.

I became an outpatient at the Cleveland Clinic in 2007. It is located right on Lake Erie. A shuttle picked me up at my hotel and took me to the hospital. Thank God, they said they'd find a doctor who wouldn't give up on me.

Just hearing the words, "We will find somebody to help you," gave me hope. I got a call four to five days later. They said, "We've found a physician. He's willing to see you." It was at the Chicago Rehab Institute, Dr. Frost. He had a good sense of humor. He helped me like they'd promised.

Complicating the situation was my blood pressure; it would drop after eating because of SMAS. My body didn't have enough fat to thrive. A lot of people have passed away after losing so much weight. It is a rare occurrence for a person to pull back and survive after dropping to a bodyweight of eighty-seven pounds.

My story has piqued people's interest. I've shared highlights and my own survival methods. I've been asked how I kept fighting despite everything. The medical community doesn't see such a fighting instinct that often from people in a condition that limits them in so many areas.

My confidence didn't return overnight — not even in ten years. It wasn't until the last twelve years, from 2008 to 2010, was when I really started developing my confidence. It started when I was selling furniture. The boss would ask me to handle something, "Take care of it," he'd say. That was how it happened. I started to develop leadership skills. As an employee in charge, I knew that I didn't have all the answers, but I made sure that we found an answer. It is better to do some damage control, clean up a mess, and appease your customer. Then, you can build back their confidence.

After that, I continued to build on that foundation of confidence.

The turning point for me was when I was able to go home following surgery for the burns. I could only sit for four hours — while doing weight shifts. To eat, I could only incline fifteen degrees maximum. I had two surgeries, *flap surgeries,* a reconstructive type of surgery. Even following healing, I am 70% more likely than the average person to have another, similar wound.

Now living back in Florida, I recently went out with some friends and celebrated the twenty-seventh anniversary of my accident. The car accident that set me on this journey.

It's a journey that I know God will be there with me every inch of the way.

I still rely on Romans 8:28.

And we know that God causes all things to work together for good to those who love God, to those who are called according to His purpose.

PART TWO

On February 4, 2018, Super Bowl LII opened with the premiere of 1Carrie Underwood's video of the song, "The Champion." Rapper Ludacris provided additional vocal talent.

The lyrics, the music, and the empowerment expressed in the pulse-pounding song have inspired me to push forward, to also be *unbreakable, unstoppable, and unshakeable.*

On 2TasteOfCountry.com, the following statement by Carrie Underwood completely explains why the song is so inspiring:

"When we were writing 'The Champion,' our main focus was to celebrate athletes at the top of their game, but we also wanted the song to resonate with people in their everyday lives," Underwood says in a press release. "We hope the lyrics will inspire people to push themselves beyond their limits to conquer anything they are trying to accomplish or overcome. There's a champion in every single one of us!"

I urge readers to Google the lyrics, buy the song, or watch the video and absorb much-needed inspiration.

9

ABOUT HOPE

GIVING UP IS EASY WHEN IT SEEMS YOU HAVE NOTHING LEFT to live for. I wasn't even twenty-one years old the day the doctor came in and told me I would have less than a 2% chance of walking again. With a few words, I felt like he'd ripped everything I had away from me. He took my dreams, my aspirations; he took my future. The wife I looked forward to having... gone; the kids in her arms would never be born. With those few words, he took my independence; he took my hope — he took my willingness to live. Everything I thought I had was taken from me in an instant. I was left empty — a shell of my former self — a broken body with nothing left to live for.

Up until then, things had always come easy to me. Whether it was in sports or school, I'd always excelled at everything I did. Now don't get me wrong, I worked really hard to make it to that point. I was fit. I was healthy. I constantly took care of myself, both body and mind. My spirit was strong, and my drive kept me going even through the darkest of moments. I was a sight to behold: handsome, athletic, kind, intelligent, and in tune with God. I was independent and strong. Even when I was lost, I knew somehow that I would find my way again. I felt that, even if I didn't always get it right, there would be a second chance for me to redeem myself.

So much for second chances.

Those first few weeks in the hospital were brutal. I stayed strong for everyone else, my parents and friends that stayed with me, but inside I was breaking. I didn't want them to worry about me, I wanted them to believe that everything was going to be okay, that I was going to be okay. However, the more I bottled up my feelings, the more I felt completely and utterly hopeless. I wasn't sharing my inner monologue with anyone. No one understood the amount of guilt I felt, the devastation I lived with.

I was in denial. I loathed myself, I blamed myself for not stopping the crash, for not telling the driver to slow down. I became hopelessly depressed, with nothing to look forward to in life besides mindless days consoling everyone else, and terrible nights begging God to change his mind, to make me whole again. No matter how hard I prayed, my prayers were left unanswered. Nothing changed. As days turned to weeks, my anger and bitterness began to bubble to the surface, and I started losing sight of myself and my faith in Him. It was when I started to blame God for what had happened, I realized I was turning into someone I wasn't.

Something needed to change.

It's easy to play the blame game. It's much easier than claiming responsibility for yourself and your actions. It is much harder to accept your situation and moving forward to find solutions, not just focus on your problems. It's much easier to stay hopeless than it is to find hope again. In a way, we enjoy feeling down and out because it gives a sense that there is nothing left to do, so we give ourselves *permission to do nothing*. The first key to recovery is revitalizing hope, starting over again from a place of clarity and strength so that you can continue to move forward on your journey.

Again, much easier said than done. It took me five weeks of misery to recognize my own deconstruction that was taking place. I was not the man I had been before the accident, either in body or mind. However, the mind is a beautiful thing. No matter where you are in life, you will always be able to control your thoughts and your mindset. That is what got me through sports as a child — when I was ready to give up after a grueling training regimen — it's what got me through being in the military, and the heartbreak of not making the BUDS program. It's what gave me the control I needed to be there for my friends and family after my accident, even though I was the one in pain.

When you recondition your mind to take responsibility for your own sense of hopelessness, it starts with understanding what hope is and how to achieve it. It also starts with an examination of your mentality, and the recognition that all the self-deprecation and fear that you harbor will *not* see you through to a better future. These first two steps are both the easiest and hardest because they come from a place of willpower. You must first believe it is possible to reach a place of hopefulness again, and then you must believe that you are capable of making it there. However, nothing fully begins until you act on it.

Let's start with hope. Hope is intangible. It's a feeling; you can't hold it or touch it or smell it. You can't experience it with your five senses — you need to feel it with your spirit and your mind. Hope is a belief system. You have to have faith in something for it to work.

Now before you say, "That's ridiculous, how do I believe in something I don't have?" I need to inform you that you will always have your mind and yourself, your essence, even when you feel like you have nothing else. When you feel hopeless, you are in a situation where you feel stuck and *believe* that nothing will turn out the way you want it to. Your belief system is based on the potential negative outcome of your circumstances. The first step in finding hope is to recognize that you capable of turning the tables by *believing in yourself and your own willpower* to battle through any of the obstacles that are thrown your way.

Believing in yourself is the only belief system that forces you to take personal responsibility for your actions and wellbeing. While believing in other systems, such as religion or society, is perfectly okay and, in fact, encouraged, believing in yourself is the only way to push past everything that is blocking your path to success.

Hope comes from believing in something that will keep you well. You can keep yourself healthy and in a positive state of mind more so than anything else. For example, after recognizing the shift in my mentality, and how it had become warped by my own negativity, I started to reevaluate my belief system. I had always believed in God, that He would help and protect me, but now that belief had been weakened considerably after weeks of begging for His forgiveness... to no result.

I still blamed Him for not fixing my legs and allowing me to walk again. I still hadn't taken responsibility for myself and my mindset. Of course, if I believed God wasn't on my side, every-thing negative that happened would just seem like another curse from the heavens. He had become the perfect excuse for my misery. I could have easily continued to believe it was His fault for putting me in a wheelchair forever, and not do anything to help myself move forward to a better future. If my belief system was based on blaming God for the results of my life, I would never have to take responsibility for my actions or inactions. I would be in the same place for the rest of my life.

To change our circumstances, we need to start doing some-thing different than what we were doing in the first place. That often starts with how we think about the world and our place-ment in it. I thought God was punishing me for something that wasn't my fault by not giving me some miracle cure that would magically give me the ability to walk again. The more I stayed in that mentality, the more bitter, miserable, and depressed I became.

Change only came when I decided to stop believing my mind's worst assumptions and start believing in myself and God again. Change only came when I took responsibility for myself and started taking steps to improve my situation. I began talking to the people around me about how I really felt. Change only came when I accepted that the only way to have a future is to believe that you can make one.

You have to take action and responsibility for yourself to have hope. No matter where you are, what life has given you, or the hand you've been dealt in life, once you take control of your own life, you will be able to accomplish anything. When you start taking positive action, hope is no longer intangible. It becomes something that you can see, feel, and touch. You can see your circumstances changing because you have taken the proper steps to ensure you move forward. You can feel yourself gaining confidence because you have faith in your abilities. You can touch those around you with your positivity and outlook on life, and inspire them with newfound hope.

Hope is more than just an abstract concept. It is a real force of being that helps us keep going in even the most trying of times. It's important to recognize that our ability to keep fighting comes from within, though it is crucial to utilize the resources around us to make sure we don't fall back into that hole of self-doubt and negativity again. Immerse yourself in an activity. Actively doing things and being social, especially if they will help your current predicament, is the best way to keep your mind off the itching negativity that will try to resurface. Participate in social gatherings, whether they are in the form of support groups or just with a bunch of your friends.

Being social helps stem the feelings of isolation that can come when you are put in a circumstance where you feel no one else understands. Don't let doubt creep in again. Remember, you are the one who controls your destiny with your outlook, mindset, and action. You also control the people you surround yourself with and what you believe in.

Don't be afraid to set healthy boundaries. If someone is making you feel like you are somehow inferior or broken because of what you have gone through, you don't need them in your life.

Believe in those who believe in you, and if you have faith in something, such as God or the universe, use the strength that gives you to believe in yourself.

We all need to believe in something to make it through life. It gives us the hope and strength we need to move forward, even when our backs are against the wall, and it seems like we have no place else to go. Believing in yourself will give you the willpower to conquer anything.

Whether you are experiencing a disability, illness, or trauma, finding hope within yourself is the first step to a brighter future. With that first step, you will be able to change not only your world — but the world around you.

10

EDUCATE YOURSELF

WHEN I WAS FIRST DIAGNOSED AS QUADRIPLEGIC, *EVERYTHING* about my life changed. It was like starting over from rock bottom – I didn't know what to do or where to begin. My whole life had turned upside down, and somehow, I had to set it back on course, and then navigate through all the obstacles in my way. I had to learn how to control my body again. I had to learn how to operate my medical equipment. I had to learn how to sleep, eat, go to the bathroom — all of which I had taken for granted before my accident.

Did you know the body of a person who has suffered a spinal cord injury is more susceptible to the dangers of high blood pressure than an able-bodied human, or that something as simple as BP doesn't work in the same way?

My injury was devastating. That's a fact. At first, I lived in a shell of my own creation; a place of insecurity, anger, and hurt. I was plagued by nightmares during those first few weeks in the hospital, with nothing but the worst of my pain to keep me company through the night. I had to navigate feelings of loss and guilt while relearning everything I thought I knew about myself. It was a struggle that I won't soon forget, but it opened my eyes to something greater. It wasn't until I started reconditioning my mind, building that mental fortitude, which gave me hope, that I realized there was a lot more to my recovery than just feeling like I *could* recover. I needed to *know* more, to understand my condition and what I could do to become as functional as possible.

After I came to the realization that this was my life, that it wasn't changing — no matter how much I prayed or tried to wiggle my toes — it was important for me to start asking questions. I was already re-engaging my spirit and finding hope wherever I could, but I still lacked something crucial: *information*. I felt that I had to take responsibility for myself and the situation I was in to move forward in life, to reach my next step. The only way I could do this was by investing in myself and utilizing my resources to learn as much as I could.

Now, back in the early 90s, hospitals didn't know much about spinal cord injuries. Of course, they knew enough to treat them, and take care of the patients that had them, but not nearly enough to satisfy the thirst for knowledge that I wanted. My goal was to research all I could to regain my sense of self and build the best version of me as physically possible. I wasn't going to give up, but I also wasn't interested in old wives' tales. I wanted practicality; I wanted answers.

It started with a certain nurse. He wasn't just a source of hope and humor in my life; he also taught me the basics of what I needed to know to survive in my condition. Whenever we weren't joking around, I would ask him questions about my injury and everything he was doing to treat it. He was patient and did a great deal of explaining to my parents and me throughout my stay at the hospital. All of his expertise was invaluable, but still my thirst for knowledge wasn't quite quenched.

By the time I was transferred to Shepherd's Spinal Center in Georgia, I had mastered the art of asking questions. I was blessed to have access to a great many doctors and specialists, most of whom I actively sought after for their advice, opinion, and expertise. As I started to know more about myself, I gained the confidence I needed to feel secure with who I was becoming after the accident. With every lesson came more and more hope. I was starting to see that there was more to my future than I had originally expected, and the future wasn't all that bad.

It has been over twenty years, and I still haven't stopped learning. As the old saying goes, "Knowledge is Power." The greatest thing I ever did was start asking questions. Once I was able to understand my situation, I was able to navigate it with a bit more clarity. I wasn't so ashamed anymore. I was able to interact with others who had been through the same kind of trauma as me, and together we were able to give each other a new foundation for hope. I wasn't alone anymore. I embraced myself. My confidence grew. It was like I had blossomed into my old-self, minus the legs.

One of the biggest keys to recovery is education. When you understand your circumstances, it gives you the power to act with a sense of clarity. Instead of giving in to the fear your mind will create based on assumption, you will be able to work your way to your goals by using proven methods of success. It will give you a sense of empowerment and control, something that is difficult to achieve after experiencing any sort of trauma. Not only will you find yourself growing in confidence when you start feeling like you have more control of your situation, but you will also start to feel hopeful as well. No matter how rare the disease, how bad the depression, how hopeless the situation, of the seven billion people in the world, there is guaranteed to be someone who has gone through or is going through the same thing or something similar. With shared experience comes the ability to communicate, with communication comes information, with information comes education.

It can be overwhelming at times to embrace all the information sent your way. Honestly, over the past twenty years, I've had to learn a lot of things that I never wanted to learn about, both about my body and myself. I never expected to be sitting in a wheelchair for the rest of my life, but I sure as hell (excuse my language) wasn't going to be sitting there absolutely helpless. I had to learn how to move my upper body again. I had to discover which physical therapies I needed to do to regain simple movement in my fingers and then actively choose to do them. No one was going to do it for me. I could have decided to be spoon-fed and waited on hand and foot, but I wanted achieve a sense of independence, and I wasn't about to give into my worst fears about being a man in his early twenties with a spinal cord injury. There are no shortcuts on the road to recovery, and sometimes we have to do things the long way to make it to our destination.

Information is your friend as long as it's practical, honest, and based on facts, otherwise, it can help you in fuel your denial and ultimately hurt you. I was once asked why I hadn't researched alternative medicine in my search for answers, invest myself in finding a cure in God or through another religion. Now don't get me wrong, I prayed to God every day for five weeks after I got into my accident, begging him to give me my life back, pleading with him to fix my condition, but after a while I had to recognize that God's plan for me wasn't to regain feeling in my legs. He couldn't change me, or *wouldn't*, I should say.

I had to embrace the situation and work out a plan for myself based on the answers I got from the people around me. If I had waited for God, I wouldn't have realized His true purpose for me was to help others through their own recovery, and teach them what I learned on my path. It is always okay to seek strength in God or through whatever you practice, but do not depend on faith alone to be the main contributor to your success. You need to take responsibility for yourself, and let that faith give you the determination to keep going.

If you constantly play the *blame game,* the only person it's going to hurt is yourself. I've said that a few times already, and I stand by it. When times get tough, it's important to work through the situation by analyzing the facts. There is information *everywhere,* and from that, knowledge to be gained. Utilize your resources to find solutions to your problem, instead of trying to make them worse. For instance, if you've lost your job and need a new one, use your phone to install free job search apps or Google who is hiring in your area instead of writing a post on Facebook about how not having a job sucks.

If you've gotten into an accident, research the do's and don'ts of recovery and *ask questions,* don't expect the doctor to tell you everything you need to know about healing. If you have gone through a traumatic experience, look for group therapy sessions to attend or meet up with someone who has worked through your circumstances and recovered. The insight of others is pivotal to your success.

"Stupid is as stupid does," are the famous words of Forrest Gump. When you're first put into a situation you've never been in before, you will be inherently ignorant to it, meaning you won't initially know what to do. Don't let that ignorance turn into stupidity. This happens when you make the choice not to reach out or look for answers. There's only so long you can let shame or fear control your life. It may seem hard at first, but breaking away from those feelings to learn how to be better is more rewarding than staying in the same place you started out in for the rest of your life. I could have laid in that bed forever if I had so chosen, but I wasn't about to let life pass me by without a chance to experience more of the world.

You may not immediately get the answers you need from the people around you and that's okay. It's your job to keep seeking those answers, even through obstacles. Don't give up, keep on searching. Your destination is understanding. It may not change your predicament, but it will change your mentality. Obviously, reading a book didn't magically give me the power to walk again, but it did teach me how to control the movement I did have. Reading a book didn't give me the power to stand up, but it gave me hope. Remember, hope is intangible, but one of the keys to recovery is turning it into something you can feel, see, or touch. Hope can come from information, and it comes from education.

Pain is inevitable, but suffering is optional. We all go through pain. It's setting the limit to your suffering that matters. This is the difference between grabbing hold of an anchor when you are drowning or grabbing a life vest. We control how far we sink into the water, no matter how murky or clear it is. Bad things happen; obstacles are put in our path, it's part of the beauty of life. How we respond to those situations is what shapes us. We can either choose to be the victim or the solution. You are responsible for your recovery; you are responsible for your suffering. How far are you going to let it hold you down?

11

PERSONAL RESPONSIBILITY AND ADVOCACY

We all have to face obstacles in life; whether they are those of our own making or those that are forced on us, it is our responsibility to choose how we will address them. You can make one of two choices: accept the obstacle before you and find a solution to surmount it, or refuse to acknowledge the importance of your role in changing your circumstances and never accomplish your goals. Personal responsibility is crucial to overcoming anything thrown your way. Accepting your ability to change the situation you're in is the first step to seeing that change become a reality.

Personal responsibility is synonymous with action: it is that act of acting on your emotions, environment, and decisions, whether good or bad; it is that act of correcting the results of the emotions, environments, or decisions you've made. Every action you make has consequences, and it's important to accept responsibility for whatever those consequences are. Not only will it give you a sense of control over the situation, but it will allow you the opportunity to overcome it. Acknowledging your contribution to the circumstances that surround you will give you the basis on which you can plan to change.

Now, I've shared my story. I've told you about my soul-crushing diagnosis. I've told you about the fear, depression, and guilt that came with it. I've relayed to you about my struggle in accepting my life had change indefinitely and that I needed to make the best of what I had left. I've told you about the highest points of my highs and the lowest points of my lows. I've given you a glimpse of what it means to act on taking responsibility for yourself despite your circumstances or trauma, but I haven't taught you how to recognize it within yourself.

There are two different types of mentalities when it comes to personal responsibility: a victim's mentality and a survivor's mentality. Victims like to play the blame game. They believe everything is happening *to* them instead of *because* of them. They allow the negative situations that form around them to continue and take no steps to improve their environment. Not only are they complicit in their own suffering, they actually revel in it, whether they know it or not. These are the type of people who like to complain about everything wrong with their life and never take the initiative to fix it. People who have a victim's mentality are examples of those who have not accepted personal responsibility.

Survivors fight for what they have. They struggle through the obstacles before them to triumph. They know how hard it will be and that, through their journey, they may suffer but, ultimately, they succeed in reaching their goals because they understand the importance of contributing to their own success. These are the type of people who stay positive and act with a steadfast nature to achieve their goals, even if they are difficult. People who see themselves as survivors have acknowledged their faults and actively work on changing their circumstances. The difference between these two mentalities is acceptance; acceptance in the situation, and acceptance of your ability to change it.

When you find yourself in a place of despair and desperation, be it physical, emotional, or mental, you may think that it is unfair and unfixable. You may question how you got to that point or why you ended up there. You may fear the possibility of never escaping the hole you find yourself in. These thoughts are common when faced with an uncertain situation, and they are all examples of adopting a victim's mentality. It's our first instinct to blame others or feel sorry for ourselves because of what has happened to us, however recognizing these thoughts is the difference between living in victimhood and negativity, and accepting personal responsibility.

A survivor's mentality comes with the acknowledgment that you may be facing a particular predicament, but you are also capable of overcoming it. Don't allow yourself to be sucked into a black hole of self-pity.

A huge part of personal responsibility is inflection. You need to understand where you stand in your own mind. You need to recognize when you're allowing yourself to think negativity, and why you may be doing so. When you take on personal responsibility, it's usually on something negative, something that has had a bad consequence that needs fixing. It's needed when things are the hardest they've ever been. You need to hold yourself accountable for your own stubborn negativity and throw that mentality out the window.

You are a survivor. You have the power to change your circumstances and overcome the difficulties that stand in your way. Whether you're recovering from addiction, trauma, abuse, or illness, accepting yourself and your strength will guide you on the right path forward. Personal responsibility is the mental fortitude that kept me strong and sane when I started my rehabilitation after the accident. It's what gave me the ability to stand tall, even though I can never stand again, and it will give you the strength to persevere even in the hardest of times.

There are always going to be people who will doubt you — whiners who don't believe in their own potential and who live in a perpetual state of victimhood. There are going to be times you will be put in a position you will wish you had never been put in, and that's okay — not because what is happening to you is okay

— but because you will ultimately learn from it and grow stronger because of it. It will spark the change inside of you and give you the conviction you need to fight for the life you've always wanted because you never want to be in that position again. Soon, it will become second nature to accept the obstacles that get thrown at you, and acknowledge what you personally need to achieve to change them.

Advocate for yourself. The only person you can *always* rely on is *you*, no matter how difficult that may seem. You always need to be your own advocate. Even with tons of support, you ultimately need to be the one who *wants* to change. When your back is against the wall, you're the only one who can decide whether to bend or break, no one else can make that decision for you. You are the only one who can keep fighting or choose to give up; to stand up tall or hide your face; to embrace your insecurities or allow them to consume you. These decisions are easier to make when you understand the power you hold in your hands by accepting personal responsibility. No one will ever be able to take that power away from you.

12

WELLNESS PLANNING

"WHEN IN DOUBT, PLAN IT OUT," AS THE SAYING GOES. WHEN my accident first happened, I had no clue what life would have in store for me. Day in and day out, doctors and nurses came and went through my room, checking gauges and monitors to make sure I was stable. Once I had passed the precipice of danger, they stopped coming in as frequently. Then, they showed my family how to care for me.

I could no longer walk. I could barely move, and I needed assistance for nearly everything I did. My mother had to help me use the bathroom as if I was a two-year-old child, not a twenty-year-old man. I was beyond mortified. Not only did I feel that my life had been taken from me, but my dignity had been stripped away, too. I wanted to be independent – I didn't want to rely on anyone else.

It took a while, but eventually, I made up my mind to do everything I could to regain control of the life that had slipped through my fingers. I've already shared with you how I developed my own form of hope, how I educated myself, how I took responsibility for my actions, and how you can do the same things too. Now I want to teach you about a crucial aspect of recovery: *planning* for it.

Wellness planning isn't a new concept. It's a tool that has been used for decades to help people overcome their fears, illnesses, and traumas. The idea is to plan for the future by identifying the things that *help you feel well* and the things that *bring you down*.

Your wellness planner essentially becomes a list of actions that you should *avoid* or *perform* conducive to your recovery. It helps guide you into staying on the right path so that you don't stray into territories that might negatively affect your progress. Just like the Bible offers guidance on the moral ins and outs of being human, your wellness planner offers guidance on how to maintain healthy boundaries and what to do if you inadvertently cross them.

The point of a wellness planner is to keep you on track mentally. That way, you can focus on your goals without the stress and interference of negative thinking or behavior. Your wellness plan can help you identify your own, personal triggers and what to do if you experience one. Your plan will also aid in identifying actions — or inactions — that help you cope and increase your positivity levels, and identify the point where you need another person to intervene to help you regain stability. This information is crucial to your recovery, and by creating a wellness plan, you essentially allow yourself an opportunity to intimately understand how your mind works. By writing down the particulars of your own plan, you're making a detailed map of your psyche and providing yourself a tool from which you can control your future.

I didn't discover wellness planning until after the accident. While in college, I was taking an advanced psychology class. It was only then that I realized what was missing from my life. I had spent all this time educating myself about my disability, learning how to treat it, and how to keep growing independently. But there were also a lot of times where I wanted to give up because deep down inside, I still felt broken. On those days, my mental fortitude would collapse and I wouldn't make any progress — not on my coursework, not on my physical therapy, and not on any of my advocacy projects. I was in a stalemate with myself and my mind.

Sometimes, an incident as simple as a person looking at me the wrong way or if I had to ask the drive-through attendant to unwrap my straw, would send me — mentally — back to square one. If those types of circumstances continued, I would descend into a dark hole, where I was worthless and nothing mattered. Those holes were hard to get out of by myself. They took a great amount of control on my part not to continue to fall any farther.

With the idea of wellness planning, I was able to connect the final piece I needed to avoid falling into another terrible hole. If I did happen to find myself in a hole, the plan guided me on how to get out of it.

I started first by identifying my triggers, the things that sent me spiraling into a bout of depression. I didn't like to feel dependent. In circumstances where I had to ask for help or even when people, albeit out of kindness, tried to help me because of my wheelchair... well, it left me feeling bad about myself.

I've thought a lot about these things and how they've affected me emotionally. With that kind of introspection, I was able to realize what would counteract those negative thoughts.

That's where the wellness planner came in. I wrote down all the things that impacted me negatively and then, right next to them, I wrote down all the positive actions I could do to fight those negative feelings.

Through this process, I learned a lot about myself, including how I let my sense of pride control my reactions and, therefore, also control my future. I also found that I wasn't doing nearly enough of the things I *actually liked doing*. That behavior, or lack of behavior, contributed to a good amount of my condition of unwellness. From there, I was able to start changing my actions so that I could live healthier and work more cohesively on my goals.

I started going out more and going to events. I had previously thought I would be shunned at these types of events because of my disability. I'd stopped caring what other people thought because I knew it was my own pride getting in the way and affecting me negatively.

My wellness planner became the foundation from which I started keeping myself accountable for the changes I wanted to see in my growth.

YOUR WELLNESS PLANNER

A good wellness planner always starts with research. You need to understand yourself intrinsically. You need to understand your emotions and what makes you feel well or unwell. You need to recognize the patterns in your life that are contributing both to negativity and positivity. Most importantly, you need to start strategizing on how to stay on the positive end of your wellness spectrum, and away from the negative, deep end.

For example, let's say you suffer from severe anxiety. Your wellness planner should have a list of things that trigger your anxiety and how to counteract them. Your triggers should be written down, so you recognize them as triggers. Oftentimes, we find ourselves questioning whether we are overreacting or having a legitimate emotional response. Without a plan, written down, you might not know definitively if you are having an anxiety attack, or if it's just your mind playing tricks on you.

It's important to understand that you are not crazy for feeling certain ways about things. However, it's also important to control your responses to those things when they do happen so that you can have a successful future. Your wellness exercises are there to remind you what helps you regain control of your mental wellbeing. Maybe you find strength in being out and around nature; one of your wellness exercises can be to go for a walk outside to calm your mind.

Perhaps drawing or painting relaxes you; when you feel yourself panicking, have your supplies on hand to start doodling until you're able to maintain a state of calm.

You might enjoy social activity, and when you don't participate in social events, it makes you feel down. You should make it a point to plan your days, so you consistently go to events with other people.

Maybe you get easily overwhelmed or stimulated, and writing helps you gather your thoughts. One of your wellness activities should be writing, and because you know you may need to write without much notice, you should always keep a pen and paper with you.

Wellness planning is mental preparation. It can be hard to keep your hope up or your mindset in the right place, especially when recovering from intense trauma. By preparing yourself for what you can and cannot handle, you are gathering your mental fortitude and identifying what you need to improve on. It's okay to not be okay, but it's not okay to let that problem hold you back. The purpose of this practice is to make sure you don't fall into those deep, dark holes that can be hard to recover from. It's also to ensure that if you do, you can find the help you need to climb out.

Everyone needs help at some point during their lifetime. We, as humans, would never have survived as long as we have without asking others for help. While a wellness planner can get you far, you should also have an accountability partner who will hold you to your recovery. This person can be a friend, a spouse, a family member, a therapist, or someone else who has been through the same trauma. The most important thing is that you trust them.

This person should know about your triggers and your wellness exercises, that way, should you fall into a hole you can't get yourself out of, and you can't remember what to do or take action, they will be able to guide you in the same way your wellness planner would. This person should also act as an intervention partner. They should be the person you call when you know that you've fallen far beyond what your wellness planner can do. They should be someone you can rely on to help you find your way back onto the correct path. However, don't mistake your accountability partner with a crutch. You shouldn't depend on them to keep yourself moving forward. They are supposed to be there as a support *if* you need it. Don't make the mistake of putting your recovery on someone else's shoulders, because you will never learn how to help yourself when you experience a dip in your emotional state. You will also likely harm or even destroy the relationship you have with that person.

Remember, we all must claim personal responsibility. You are responsible for your mental wellbeing. You control whether you get better or not, whether you recover or not, whether you grow or not. Everyone else is a support to help you through this journey, not travel the journey for you.

That being said, you have the power to control your destiny. If you plan for your goals accordingly and understand how to take care of yourself when the time comes, you won't need to ever rely on anyone else. You will be able to continue prospering on your own volition. You will be able to succeed with your own hands. You will be able to accomplish things that you never thought possible because it was *you* who put the effort and time to make it happen.

You now have the tools to make it happen; it's time to start working for it.

13

MINDSET

THE MIND IS A POWERFUL THING. IT CONTROLS EVERYTHING we do or don't do; every action, every movement, every decision we make happens because we first thought it. It has been scientifically proven that the way you think controls how your future will take shape based on your actions. You can change the outcome of almost every situation you face by just using the power of your mind. You have the ability to decide who you are, what you do, and where you want to be. I may not be able to move my legs, but I have the power of my words and thoughts to build positive environments and live a fulfilling life. I am blessed to have the most important part of being that I will ever need, and so are you.

Being human comes from having a mind. Your body is a shell. You can be the most physically in shape, but if you're mentally weak, if your mindset isn't right, you won't make it through the most difficult of challenges. This can apply to anything from climbing a mountain to taking a critical exam. I saw it when I was an athlete, I saw it in the military, and I lived it after my accident. In order to succeed, you need to persevere, and in order to persevere, you must have the right mindset.

I've found that the best mindset to have is one of open-mindedness, positivity, and patience. You will never reach your full potential with a negative mindset.

It can only be accessed by treating yourself with care, understanding your weaknesses, and utilizing your strengths to overcome adversity. By embracing your inner being with all its flaws and successes, you will start recognizing your inherent power and resilience. You will start to believe in yourself, and most importantly, believe it's possible to change your circumstances. Don't look at what you're lacking as weakness, look at it as something to improve on, something to grow.

When you adopt a positive mindset, you have the power to create a healthy, understanding environment for yourself and those around you. Similarly, the opposite is also true. When you constantly self-deprecate, think negatively, and believe in the worst of others, you are creating a world of conflict and chaos. You will never be able to thrive in this unhealthy atmosphere. Even your physical environment can change with the right mindset because now you're looking for solutions to leave the toxicity around you and build something better for yourself. If you continually think that you will never be able to get out of the mess you're in, I'm sorry to say — you won't. If you start believing in yourself and your inherent ability to grow and overcome, you will see your problems melt away because you are acting on solving them with a critical eye on your goals.

When I had my accident, I had two choices: give in to my darkest thoughts and feelings or push through my pain and try to create something better for myself. We all know which one I chose. I wasn't content with the idea of living in a wheelchair for the rest of my life *and* being a dependent, angry, bitter man whose outlook on living was beyond depressing. Without acting on the positive mental fortitude I had rebuilt by changing my mindset, I wouldn't have bothered learning how to feed myself or drive; I wouldn't have bothered going to school or starting a foundation; I wouldn't have bothered writing this book and trying to help others. It wouldn't matter because I would be trapped in the same hole of negativity that kept me down during the hell that was those first five weeks after finding out I would never walk again.

It takes time to adapt to new circumstances, especially if they are hard. Maybe you are suffering trauma or a loss; maybe you are suffering from illness; maybe you are battling addiction. Regardless, these things can be worked through and resolved when you have a good understanding of yourself and can objectively interpret your circumstances. This will give you the opportunity to establish goals that are within your reach so you may change where you are and what you are doing with your life. It's easy to see the glass as half-empty when life puts obstacles in your way, especially if they seem insurmountable, but remember: you have the power to create hope, you have the power to channel change, and you have the power of a positive mindset on your side.

If you shut down and tell yourself that this is something that you can't do, you won't be able to do it. If you tell yourself you won't get better, and you take no steps to make yourself better, you aren't going to change. If you keep putting yourself down and making excuses for your shortcomings instead of actively working on them, you will always be incapable of surmounting the challenges you face. Trust me, the quadriplegic man who has devoted his life to teaching others how to overcome their greatest adversities: *you need to start looking at the glass as half-full.* That way, when someone pours in your cup, you'll appreciate it far more, and enjoy a refreshing drink.

- Stop letting yourself get in the way of your success.
- Stop letting others determine whether or not you are capable of succeeding.
- Stop letting your environment control you.

People like to use their pain as a crutch or an excuse. It gives them something to fall back on when they aren't successful.

They have something they can blame it on. They become comfortable in their own suffering because it means that they never have to achieve anything more than what they already have. You need to stop allowing yourself to get sucked back into that cycle of negativity. Your fear of failure is far more detrimental than failing itself. If you don't take chances, if you don't allow yourself to leave your dark bubble of comfort, you will never be able to experience anything different than the life you are living now. I could have easily decided not to try new things because of my disability. Most people aren't going to question a guy in a wheelchair. I could have chosen to live in my bubble of vulnerability and insecurity, but I wanted to propel myself past my weaknesses, shortcomings, and doubts by moving forward and learning from them instead.

The walls you build aren't protecting you, they are caging you in a world of turmoil. You need to break those walls down. When you build walls, it may seem like you're keeping bad things out, but the truth is you're also not letting good things in, and all the anger and fear you keep behind those walls *stay with you.* You need to start accepting your past, including your failures and shortcomings, so you can use it to better your life. With a positive mindset that is open to learning from past mistakes, and willing to do whatever it takes to make it, you will succeed.

That's not to say it doesn't take work to change your mindset. It takes determination and perseverance. You must resolve to constantly and consistently correct your thinking when it strays into negativity. I challenge you to try this: whenever you feel bad about yourself or you think that you won't be able to accomplish your goals, identify three positive aspects of your life and focus on those. In this way, you are training your brain to recognize the good far outweighs the bad. Don't be afraid to let your creativity loose. Do whatever you can to create a stable pattern of positivity in your life. If you find yourself behaving too self-critically, balance those thoughts by also giving yourself praise for something you've done well.

To achieve a positive mindset, you must believe it's possible and *make it happen*. Remember, we create our own hope by making it tangible. You have all the resources at your disposal to educate your mind, to teach yourself, to build a foundation of growth in your life. You don't need to hide behind your fears anymore, you need to start letting go and embracing all that you are. Break free from the disappointment, sorrow, and doubt you hold in your heart. Once you realize that you are capable of overcoming adversity, you will do just that.

Stay focused on your goals. Be creative. Be positive. If you get stuck in a rut, use your resources to climb out. Don't let your pride cloud your growth. If it's the fear or embarrassment of reaching out that keeps you from doing so, you need to recognize that you are keeping yourself from seeking the help you need to grow. That's the beginning of changing your mindset: recognizing the things you do that hold you back and changing those behaviors. The only way to change is understanding what needs to be changed and actively working on it. Take personal responsibility for your mental health and mindset. *You* are the one who has the power to make anything happen. You just have to want it first.

I believe you are capable of changing your circumstances, of overcoming your pain, of forging a new future for yourself. You have all the knowledge and tools at your disposal to do so. All you need now is the ambition to achieve it. With that resolve, you will be able to accomplish your wildest dreams. Embrace your past to secure your future. Learn from your mistakes; don't think of them as failures, but as learning experiences. With every failure comes the knowledge to succeed next time. I want you to live in profound positivity, even when things are hard. I encourage you to take a deeper look at yourself and those around you, to identify what needs to change and make it happen. The only one who will always have your back is yourself. Take advantage of that.

We've all heard that the definition of insanity is doing the same thing over and over again and expecting different results. Your mindset is the difference between staying the same forever, getting worse, or improving. You need to be the change you want to see in your life. You can be the change you want to see in your life. If you believe you can accomplish it and you take action towards accomplishing it, you will succeed, even if you have to fail a hundred different times first. It's time to start setting your goals because your time has arrived. Don't miss it.

14

MAKIN' IT HAPPEN

BACK WHEN I WAS FINISHING MY TWO-YEAR DEGREE IN college, I had a program director approach me. She told me I needed to finish my four-year degree so that her team could hire me as a teacher. She believed that I would be a strong addition to the school and a great benefit to its students. I laughed in her face; not out of cruelty, I could never do that, but out of sheer disbelief. I thought she had the wrong man. There was no way I could teach other people, especially since I had failed at so much in the past. I politely declined her offer and carried on with my life. Ironically, twenty-something years later, teaching others is exactly what I'm doing now with this book.

That being said, as I write this chapter, I'm celebrating the twenty-seventh anniversary of my accident. I would say it's bitter-sweet, but that's a lie. I'm happy to be alive, and today is a reminder that every day we are blessed to have on this earth should be cherished. To me, it's a rebirth of sorts. I'm not the same as I once was but that's okay. We're always changing, always growing, and always moving forward. Such is life.

On the day of the anniversary, I decided to take several hours to reflect on my life. I spent the afternoon enjoying the water at

Clearwater Beach, Florida. If you've never been there, the sand is white and feels like powder, while the water is kind of murky bluish-green, due to the continental shelf, a sloping sea floor unique to the Gulf of Mexico.

Clearwater Beach is beautiful and warm; tourists wander the boardwalk aimlessly, taking snapshots of their lives, and fishermen cast their lines out into the sea. The best time to visit is just before dusk when the sun is low in the sky, but the air is still warm. This is how I found myself on the pier, staring at the waves crashing against the shoreline. I wanted to reflect on the last twenty-seven years of my life, how I had changed, what I had accomplished, and what I could learn from it. I've decided the following: *Life is a celebration*.

Every day that you get to walk this earth is a miracle. Even when times get tough and things don't go your way, the sun always rises and so will you. We may not have tomorrow, but we have today to make a difference in our lives and in the lives of those around us. By choosing to focus on the positive instead of the negative, you are setting yourself up to appreciate the beauty of life and all its experiences.

I choose to focus on the positive things in my life; I value the time I have and look at it with gratitude. I feel blessed to be here, especially since I could easily have not. I may not be able to walk, but my life isn't bad. It's far from it. It's amazing! I've achieved independence. I can drive. I have friends. I travel frequently. I take full advantage of my days and enjoy my nights. I love life and I'm living the best one I could possibly have because it's the only one I'll ever get. If you had asked me about this twenty-seven years ago, I probably wouldn't have felt the same. That's the point I want to make to you. You may not have it all now, but you *will*. You *will* overcome. You *will* succeed. You *will* live a life of prosperity.

Reflecting on the beach I was able to realize my faults, but also understand how I can improve in my future. Life isn't about the things that happen to you, it's about how you respond to them. I realized that you will always be setting yourself up for failure if you only look at the bad in life. You won't be able to succeed or achieve because you're too focused on something else. I've long since realized that I can't use my body the way I used to. It used to *pain* me that I could no long destress by working-out or doing some sort of physical activity. I used to focus on how much that *hurt me*, even though the solution was right in front of my eyes. Instead of crying over what I had lost, I could find something else that would allow me that same relaxation that I used to enjoy. The same goes for any problem. If you are too focused on the problem, you will never find the solution.

The mind is the most powerful part of your body. It can help you achieve anything you hope for, but it can also keep you in a dark, unpleasant place if you so choose.

- Don't live in the past.
- Don't agonize over your mistakes and failures.
- Don't let the things you've experienced in life hold you back from new experiences.

Stay present-minded — stay in the here and now. Now, that doesn't mean to resist change, it means to keep moving forward. Yesterday was yesterday and tomorrow will be tomorrow. Remember that all your mistakes are lessons from which you can learn. They are reasons to grow. Leave your past behaviors in the past but use the lessons you've learned to keep moving forward. Choose to focus on building a healthy lifestyle for yourself each day. It will keep you grounded and focused on your goals so that you can overcome any situation that might present itself at the time. Prepare yourself for the future by setting up resources daily that promote growth. Today is the day to determine your path for tomorrow. Don't allow negativity to fester and create an atmosphere that advocates for failure.

I want you to realize you have more potential locked inside of you than what you think. No matter how small or insignificant that may seem to you at this moment in time, I would like you to think about it like Legos. Legos are building blocks. You must start building from the bottom. Even when you feel like a failure, you still have the potential inside of you to grow. It's like the saying that goes, "When they buried me, they didn't know I was a seed." You are a seed that has just been planted but is ready to sprout. You are a single Lego block that is waiting to be built on. The trials and tribulations you face are the foundation from which you will grow and blossom. Every decision that you make is not in vain as long as you learn something from it, whether positive or negative. Each lesson offers a new perspective from which you can grow. As long as you keep learning with an open and positive mind, it will always be worth it.

We all suffer. We all go through pain. We all have baggage and trauma. It's inevitable. The difference between making it and breaking it is whether you will allow everything you've been through to hold you back or propel you forward. I've said this before, and I will say it one more time: don't play the blame game. You have the resources at your disposal to work through any challenge you face and make it to the other side with a smile on your face. And smile wide, with pride, and your chin held high because you made it and you deserve all the praise and positivity that comes from taking matters into your own hands and not letting your trauma define you indefinitely.

Take control of your destiny. Congratulate yourself on small wins. Forgive yourself because God knows that no one is perfect. Make a commitment to yourself that you will start being the change you want to see in your life. Write down the things you like and *do those things*. Don't let life pass you by because it will if you let it. Have patience. A tree doesn't grow overnight but it will stand tall for hundreds of years, and no matter how many leaves fall from its branches, they will always grow back. Remember to keep an open mind. The only path to change is understanding, and the only path to understanding is learning. Never stop learning about yourself. Make sure to find the time to sit on a pier (or your front porch) during a warm summer evening and reflect on all the hours you have spent on this Earth.

The world is more beautiful than it is cruel. Remember to laugh. The Bible says that laughter is the best medicine, and I tend to believe that. Even on your worst days, in those moments where your emotions are raw, when you feel empty inside, try to find something that makes you laugh. You need to have humor in your life because it reminds you that you are *alive*.

I wrote this book because I wanted to empower you into taking action. I want you to recognize your strengths and grow from your weaknesses. I don't want you to let your circumstances hold you back, no matter how terrible or difficult they are. I want you to embrace your past, but not allow your trauma to control your future. I want you to actively participate in society. I want you to whole-heartedly enjoy your life and understand that it is *worth* living, no matter the struggle you are facing now. I want you to step outside your comfort zone: dance, sing, go skydiving, travel to a different country, learn a new language, go back to school, do the little things that will give you a sense of freedom and positivity, even in your darkest moments. I want these things for you because it is what I wish I had wanted for me twenty-seven years ago.

You've been through the fires of hell but you will come out the other side. You've walked in the valley of the shadow of death, but you will survive. You have a power inside you that is so strong it can move mountains, if only you reached for it. You have a strength inside of you that comes from all your experiences and will only make you stronger. Once you access your sheer will to succeed, you will be unstoppable. You already hold the key to success, it's time that you've turned it. Only you can find your purpose and use it to rise from the ashes like a phoenix. You are unique and inherently powerful. Tap into that power and use it to set yourself free.

I believed in my strength, it's time you believed in yours.

ABOUT THE AUTHOR

Mike Wilson currently lives in Tampa Bay, Florida as he continues his medical treatment and regularly attends church. Originally from West Virginia, his Florida life includes music, watching sports, visiting the beach, and being out in the sunshine. He also enjoys socializing with friends as much as possible.

He is available for motivational speaking engagements. He may be contacted through Facebook at https://www.facebook.com/michael.wilson.370515 or email him at rollinmike93@gmail.com.

f facebook.com/michael.wilson.370515

BIBLIOGRAPHY

CHAPTER 1

1"The story of Tim Tebow's 'Promise' speech inspiring the 2008 Florida Gators | College GameDay," YouTube video, 4:33, ESPN College Football, September 29, 2018, https://www.youtube.com/watch?v=kI44yk9TSdI.

CHAPTER 3

1"PersianGulfWars."*TheColumbiaElectronic Encyclopedia,* 6th ed. Copyright © 2012, Columbia University Press. All rights reserved on InfopleaseÂ© 2000-2017 Sandbox Networks, Inc., publishing as Infoplease. 1 August 2019 https://www.infoplease.com/encyclopedia/history/asi a-africa/middle-east/persian-gulf-wars

CHAPTER 4

1HSE, S. (2017). *"Alcohol Hurts Your Mental Health"* [online] TheJournal.ie. Available at: https://www.thejournal.ie/feel-low-after-drinking- 3356911-Apr2017 / [Accessed 8 Aug. 2019].

PART 2

1 Carrie Underwood, Ludacris, "The Champion," track #13 on *Cry Pretty*, Capitol Nashville, 2018, compact disc.

2 Hermanson, Wendy, "Carrie Underwood Kicks Off Super Bowl LII With Sexy 'Champion' Video," Taste of Country, February 4, 2018, https://tasteofcountry.com/carrie-underwood-super- bowl-lii-champion-video/